PHIL JOHNSON

Phil Johnson is a music critic for the *Independent* and *Independent On Sunday*. He has lived in Bristol since 1980 and as a video film-maker documented the early days of the hip-hop and graffiti art scene out of which so many Bristol artists have emerged.

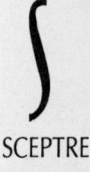

SCEPTRE

STRAIGHT OUTA BRISTOL

MASSIVE ATTACK, PORTISHEAD, TRICKY AND THE ROOTS OF TRIP-HOP

BY

PHIL JOHNSON

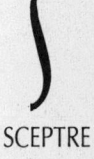

SCEPTRE

First published in 1996 by Hodder and Stoughton
First published in paperback in 1997 by Hodder and Stoughton
A division of Hodder Headline PLC
A Sceptre paperback

British Library Cataloguing in Publication Data
Johnson, Phil
    Straight outa Bristol: Massive Attack, Portishead, Tricky
    and the roots of trip-hop
    1. Rock Music - England - Bristol
    I Title
781. 6'6'0942393

ISBN 0 340 675217

Design and computer page make up
Tony & Penny Mills

Printed in Great Britain by
Mackays of Chatham PLC, Chatham, Kent

Hodder and Stoughton
A division of Hodder Headline PLC
338 Euston Road
London NW1 3BH

FOR ALICE, WITH MUCH LOVE

ACKNOWLEDGMENTS

Thanks to Simon Prosser; everyone at Venue, especially John Mitchell and Dave Higgitt; Robert Del Naja, Mark Stewart, Miles Johnson, Adrian Utley, Steve Haley, Nick Coleman, Ben Thompson, Sheryl Garratt, Marc Crewe, Campbell Stevenson, Bob Jones, Oli Timmins, Sapphire, Charles Stewart, Beezer, Paul Johnson, Steve Symons, Marc Picken, Andrew Vowles, Paul Box, and everyone who agreed to be interviewed.

While every effort has been made to obtain permission from the photographers and copyright holders of the marvellous pictures used in this book, I apologize to anyone who has not been contacted in advance or credited, and hope that they will get in touch.

CONTENTS

INTRODUCTION

Dance music that you actually listen to; hip-hop beats whose customary urgency is deconstructed into dreamy, erotic soundscapes; machine-made rhythms chock full of body, heart and soul; lyrics that transcend tired genre conventions to respond playfully to language by shooting the breeze, passing the buck, taking the piss.

Just listen to Massive Attack's song 'Blue Lines', on the album of the same name. Hear the whispered draw on a spliff pull back the curtain on a world where the usual social-documentary-as-cartoon tropes of rap dissolve into ambiguous, witty, lines that overtake one another in a dizzying crosstalk of overheard conversation. And then they stop, to be followed, after the briefest beat, by the divine retro-soul of 'Be Thankful For What You've Got'. There can be few conjunctions in popular music so good, so sensual, so fulfilling. Before you have time to reflect, the skittering Studio-One rhythms of 'Five Man Army' take over, introducing what is to be the highest point of British rap thus far: ordinary English voices summoning up a dark, rumbling story whose point is suddenly interrupted by the languorous reggae drawl of Horace Andy, taking the song back home to Jamaica. And then the epic soul of 'Unfinished Sympathy', the string orchestra sawing away against Shara Nelson's impassioned singing of 'a soul without a mind, with a body without a heart', before rising into a wonderfully overblown crescendo and then dying away again into pure sound.

The Adoration of the Magi –
the three original members
of the Wild Bunch at the
Dug Out in 1983. From
left: Miles Johnson, Nellee
Hooper, Grant Marshall
(*photo*: Beezer)

Even without the marvellous 'Daydreaming', which follows, and the glorious 'Hymn of the Big Wheel', which closes the album, this must be one of the greatest sequences in all of popular music, bar none. You can listen to it over and over again and it just keeps getting better, as the rhythms are internalized, the vocals second-guessed by the listener, the material in the grooves revealing more and more information each time.

And this was supposed to be dance music, an address to the body rather than the mind, functional rhythms providing an accompaniment to swaying bodies in a club, or to foot-tapping Kwik-Fit fitters tuned in to the dance station as they worked. It's one of the biggest cons in the discourses of popular music that real significance is accorded only to those artists who court it most assiduously, the seriousness of rock continually posed against the hip flippancy of R&B and dance music. Thus Bob Dylan and Bruce Springsteen are celebrated as artists and poets, while Marvin Gaye or Smokey Robinson remain genre performers, rising, admittedly, above the common or garden artists of their ilk, but never attaining the respect due to white boys with guitars and pained expressions.

Massive Attack's *Blue Lines* helps to answer the rock critics. It may even be, as has been claimed, the best album of the last ten years. By introducing the rapper Tricky, and Portishead's Geoff Barrow (who acted as an apprentice tape operator on the recording), *Blue Lines* also laid the foundations for what was to follow: a generation of 1990's artists who have come to define the new face of intelligent pop/dance music. Portishead's *Dummy*, and Tricky's *Maxinquaye* deepened the sense that something really new and important was happening in British music, that the normal boundaries between rock and soul, and the mutually exclusive worlds of indie and dance, were being dissolved. And it came, strange though it may seem, straight out of Bristol, the only city in the UK never to have made a significant contribution to pop's great heritage, bar a rinky-dink Russ Conway tune or two.

It came too, mainly from non-musicians, people who hadn't studied an instrument or played in a band, from DJs and bedroom-mirror rappers who were fans first and foremost, and who had learned their skills from sound-system parties and patient listening to the new sounds of American hip-hop, which were received not just as music but as part of a whole integrated sub-culture of beats and attitude, art and dance. Importantly, these were mostly people whose early adolescence was lived out in the aftermath of punk and the optimistic racial fusion of two-tone: people whose black, white and mixed-race roots had begun briefly to lose their bearings, so that even the unusually thorough segregation imposed by their quietly prosperous, impeccably ghettoized city was suddenly loosened in a few renegade clubs and party scenes, to allow the different and separate backgrounds to mix as one (or so, as we will see, the theory goes).

Their early efforts didn't take place in a vacuum either; the post-punk disarray of new-wave culture meant that odd, unassimilable pockets of bohemian defiance had taken hold, even in Bristol, where political punks like the Pop Group had begun to cross the genre frontiers and seek out examples of 'otherness' to match their own mighty sense of alienation. And in Bristol, reggae was already there, courtesy of the Jamaican immigrants who had followed the old slave-trade routes that the maritime city was so famous for back to their source. Weird avant-garde jazz was well established too: Bristolian Keith Tippett - in his own words 'the Courtney Pine of 1969' - had decamped to London at the end of the sixties to take inspiration from South African exiles the Blue Notes (whose drummer Louis Moholo would later play with Neneh Cherry in Rip Rig and Panic). His home-town acolytes soldiered on in co-ops and collectives, emerging in the jazz revival of the mid-eighties, along with incomers like the saxophonist Andy Sheppard, as part of the most happening jazz city in the country. The thriving local pub-rock and R&B scene had led to the setting up of a number of recording studios and the city's distance from London (120 miles) was just enough to ensure that a strong regional identity existed, while remaining sufficiently close to maintain links with the latest trends. There was also a record shop, Revolver, in Clifton's Triangle, where the racks teemed with the latest reggae and punk releases and featured a compendium of the best in African-American jazz and sundry, unclassifiable weirdness. Cynically, you could look back and say that yes, all the elements for the Bristol sound were in place long before it emerged; all it had needed really, was the turbocharge of hip-hop, and some kind of massive social upheaval, which it got, big time, in the St Paul's riot of 1980.

What could be called a little renaissance of Bristol music – if there had been anything to recover in the first place – began to emerge around the time of the riot, with the jazzy, funky bands like Pigbag, Rip Rig and Panic, Maximum Joy and Scream and Dance (the Clifton bands as they were known locally, after the city's posh suburb) achieving a level of success that, for the time and the place, was quite remarkable. When the first strains of American hip-hop were heard shortly afterwards, and the film *Wild Style* actually showed kids how to make that music and paint that graffiti, the club and party scenes that were eventually to give rise to the Wild Bunch, Smith and Mighty, Massive Attack and their friend Tricky, were in place. The rest, as they say, is history, though an awful lot of it is also hype.

By the beginning of 1996, when I was commissioned to write this book, mentions of 'The Bristol Sound' were everywhere, and the concept was even in danger of becoming a mite passé. Stubbornly though, the Bristol sound held on (although by now there was, of course, a lot of press interest invested in it) and the buzz continued to buzz. By the spring of 1996, on the day I'm writing this, the *Independent*'s and *Guardian*'s pop pages contain three separate references to Massive Attack; one noting that Tina Turner's new album features a version of 'Unfinished Sympathy'; one checking them as the cause of Everything But the Girl's renewed popularity (Tracey Thorn was a guest singer on *Protection*); and one recalling the band's 1991 remix of a track by the Pakistan Sufi singer Nusrat Fateh Ali Khan.

By this point the dark spectre of trip-hop had also arrived on the scene. An unappealing term coined by *Mix-Mag* magazine to describe the new breed of slowed-down and dubbed-up hip-hop-derived music that the success of Massive Attack, Tricky and Portishead had given rise to, trip-hop was suddenly everywhere. It could be found in the post-rave aesthetic of blunted beats put out by bedroom mixers like those on James Lavelle's Mo-Wax label, or in the work of Leftfield, the Chemical Brothers and too many white dub warriors to mention. A convenient label whose drug reference point proved irresistible (although the drug it implied was, of course, the wrong one) trip hop became an all-purpose marketing term and even though the Bristol bands might resent it, it didn't stop Massive Attack's record company licensing a track for a *This is Trip Hop* compilation album, on the basis, I suppose, of any port in a storm. To be fair, the term does help in identifying what has become a new genre of dance music (the kind, of course, that you don't dance to), and in enumerating the enormous influence the Bristol sound was having.

For a while the styles of Massive, Tricky and Portishead seemed to be more or less occupied by the advancing trip-hop armies, and written about as if the two things were interchangeable, although a key point in arguing for their exclusivity would have to be that the Bristol boys tend to favour songs while trip-hop proper goes for long, dreamy loops that perhaps almost anyone with the necessary equipment and an extended tolerance for sampling could eventually come up with. Ironically, the two paths meet up in the latest form of Bristol music to become successful: the brilliant sound collages of drum and bass producers like Roni Size, Krust and Flynn and Flora, whose own roots go right back to the days when the first wave of home-grown hip-hop was emerging, once again reinforcing the idea of a Bristol sound as something special.

But when I first began approaching people to get interviews for this book, the Bristol sound became one that dare not speak its name. When I rang Caroline Killoury of Fruit, the management company for Tricky, Portishead and previously for Massive, she was hardly encouraging. The Bristol bands did not, it seemed, like being associated with Bristol or with each other. But they come from Bristol, I said, they've recorded together, and they're associated enough to share the same management company in you; there's even the same samples, even the same tracks, on their albums. Indeed, if you were Pete Frame researching a rock family tree you could start right here at Fruit, at the company founded by Caroline Killoury who formerly worked with Neneh Cherry's husband at Cherry's management company, Cherry Bear. Cherry had been a member of Rip Rig and Panic, having a child with their drummer, Bruce Smith, who went to school with the Wild Bunch's Miles Johnson; the Wild Bunch got their first breaks through Cherry's contacts with *The Face* magazine; members of Massive worked on Cherry's *Raw Like Sushi* album; Cameron got them their deal with Virgin, superintended the *Blue Lines* album, enrolled Geoff Barrow to work on the next Neneh album; Fruit recommended Portishead to Go!-Disc records, signed Portishead and Tricky to a management deal, along with Massive Attack before they left …

'Personally, I can see what you're saying but I wouldn't hold out much hope. Why don't you write me a letter setting out your plans and I'll send it on to them?'

I wrote the letter but nothing happened and I slowly became conscious of what every writer for the press eventually gets to know about the PR industry; that when there's a product to sell they'll wine you, dine you and slime you, send you across the world first-class, no expense spared; but when there's no immediate selling point or it simply doesn't serve their purposes, they couldn't give a toss, and even the famously bubbly telephone manner can get a little tetchy. For a while it looked as if the book would have to proceed like a Nick Broomfield documentary, where the director's pursuit of an interview with Mrs Thatcher, say, or Eugene Terre Blanche, is inevitably stymied and the film maker is reduced to making a film about the non-event that ensues, full of close-ups of telephones and overheard conversations with functionaries, following the improbable characters who well up in the wake of the principal girl or boy's reluctance to get involved.

There were other reasons for the lack of enthusiasm many of the principal players held for the project, some noble, some less so. They were doubtless sick to death of the Bristol sound tag and the provincialism it implied; Portishead and Tricky had been written about probably too much already, and at a ludicrously early stage of their careers. There was also lots of bad feeling and jealousy between some of the artists, and between them and their less successful peers in Bristol.

With Massive Attack, one had to proceed by oblique strategies. They weren't keen and like a supplicant to the Godfather, I first had to approach intermediaries, assure them of my good intent, and at length a meeting was arranged with Robert Del Naja, whom I knew slightly from years ago. Once convinced that the project was going to happen anyway, and encouraged by his management, he agreed to talk and became briefly very excited about the idea; indeed for a while he was interested in designing the cover of the book. Actually getting him to talk, however, or anyone else come to that, proved difficult and the Bristol myth of a group of people who get up sometime early in the afternoon, light the first spliff of the day shortly afterwards and then spend the remainder of their time avoiding all known forms of work, seemed suddenly and uncomfortably close to home. At last we did talk, and I also interviewed the usually silent Mushroom (Andrew Vowles). The third member, Daddy G (Grant Marshall) remained recalcitrant. Speaking on the phone from his bath one afternoon, with, as like as not, I thought, curls of smoke rising decoratively over the tile work as he talked, he wasn't, he said, sure about it. I had once written that the band's dub album was more like Fred Perry than Lee Perry, a cheap shot that had irritated him, and he had taken offence.

Meanwhile, as the principal protagonists dallied, I was approached by others, who, like the Peter Lorre character in a Warner Brothers thriller of the forties, sidled into my gumshoe's office, possibly in disguise, and made outlandish claims. Others intimated that there were things one didn't really want to know, that it was even dangerous to speak of, dark secrets of a criminal nature, drugs, guns and gangster business. People called up, from New York, from Japan, and the plot thickened, the mythic dimensions of the story beginning to come together. There were all the characters for a classic *Golden-Bough* style ritual tale: the king over the water (Miles Johnson, the leader of the original Wild Bunch, now in New York); the pretender who had stolen his throne (the producer Nellee Hooper, by far the most successful of the old firm); the old sage (Mark Stewart), and poor children who had been cast out or even eaten by their parents (too numerous to mention). There were various warring tribes, who lived by raiding the treasure houses of rival record companies; a new generation of young pretenders with their eyes on the prize; Wagnerian slaves in the underworld mines, forced to dig up riffs to be used by their masters, and a growing band of the dispossessed, the I–could–have–been– a–contenders, the wannabes or also-rans who went to the same parties, took the same drugs but somehow failed to get the same chance.

Again reinforcing the mythic context, and emphasizing the fact that there was, after all, a Bristol sound and a history to document, was the memory of an event. In July of 1985 the Arnolfini Gallery in Bristol put on a show of graffiti art, the artists – including 3D (Del Naja, later of Massive Attack), spraying directly on to the gallery walls. The work was perhaps a little disappointing, its raw energy losing something between the institutional context and the rather porous character of the gallery walls, but for one night the Wild Bunch were invited to put on a jam in the main downstairs gallery, and I video-taped it for the Arnolfini's archive. Looking at the tape now is documentary evidence that the Bristol sound exists. There, gathered around the turntables, was the Wild Bunch: Miles Johnson and Nellee Hooper cutting up tracks, Grant Marshall picking out the next record as a very young Mushroom stands by his shoulder looking on. Claude Williams (Willie Wee) and 3D are on the mike. In the audience are Mark Stewart and Gary Clail, Smith and Mighty, Tricky, and, on his first trip to Bristol from his home in the commuter town of Portishead without his mum, the barely adolescent Geoff Barrow.

Though the Arnolfini jam wasn't the real thing, like the club dates and warehouse parties of the same period, the tape provides a powerful reminder of just how important those early days were. The gallery is packed out with kids who had never been there before – the show set a record in attendance over its month-long run – and it's a vivid testimony to the popularity of the hip-hop culture of the time, full of break-dancing a-go-go, sportswear clothing and sweaty, bug-eyed youth. Occasionally, a group of adult Arnolfini regulars walks past the camera, like safari-jacketed anthropologists on a field trip.

The making of the tape – which I did partly for the Gallery and partly for a Master's thesis – is also relevant to the story of the Bristol sound, and of what might be called the blagging aesthetic that has characterized so much of its history. As a lecturer at a local college, with a role that involved looking after the audio visual studio, I used to teach Del Naja's girlfriend and, after meeting him around the time of the Arnolfini jam, he would come into college and I would help him to edit his growing collection of tapes. These were mainly the equivalent of a cuttings file, featuring appearances he had made on various local news and views programmes about graffiti, for he was already a noted artist with several high-profile sites and a couple of arrests to his name. On the first occasion, we intercut excerpts from these sources with shots from his copy of *Taxi Driver* and a home video of a Wild Bunch jam at a local club, the Granary, into a rough scratch video of the sort popular at the time. When the next term started he enrolled on an art course in order to continue to use the equipment and he began to make a film. He blagged equipment from me, assembled a cast and went about the exercise with the vigour of Scorsese himself. When it came to editing he was a perfectionist, working for weeks over the short, five-minute-or-so piece, starting from scratch again and again, fiddling with the ancient mixer to get exactly the right quality of grainy black and white. It became something of an obsession as he went on and on without the piece ever seeming to be finished.

Shortly afterwards, again for my dissertation, I made a film of the Wild Bunch at the St Paul's flat shared by Miles Johnson and Grant Marshall, featuring Miles and Nellee cutting up tracks on the Technics double decks. At the end of the day's filming, I gave Hooper a lift to his home in the working-class estate of Barton Hill, he blagging it by not saying where he wanted to go, but pretending it was just around the corner, going 'left, right, just a bit further', until we reached the destination. This notion of blagging –

getting resources by dint of subterfuge - was there from the beginning and the Wild Bunch progressed by similar stratagems throughout its short life, blagging work on television documentaries about the British hip-hop and graffiti scene, blagging a trip to Japan, blagging record companies, blagging the style press of *The Face* (an early and very significant supporter) until Hooper had, no doubt, blagged himself into Soul to Soul, Miles Johnson into fashion modelling and the others, eventually, into work with Neneh Cherry and a deal with Virgin.

They would probably have achieved all this anyway, but the blagging aesthetic remains of paramount importance in trying to assess how the Bristol sound came about. They didn't get where they are today by simply being a fruit on a tree just waiting to be picked. No, they blagged it, and perhaps that's why they are so wary of being blagged themselves.

And along the way, of course, there was some serious falling-out. Blaggers were, in turn, blagged or turned over in the pursuit of further blagging opportunities and that's partly why the notion of a handy, catch-all Bristol sound does not go down well with many of the participants. There are skeletons in the closet, dark doings in the past and many of the principal players are no longer on speaking terms. There are questions of authorship too; of who did what and for what reward, which recall the kinds of music-biz practice of the fifties R&B days, when the names on the music publishing agreement did not always match the identities of those who actually created the song. In the age of the digital sampler, this becomes even more complicated and the disputes begin to resonate with the history of the city of Bristol itself where the poet Thomas Chatterton, the marvellous boy - a Tricky for his age - palmed off his verses as the surviving manuscripts of a bygone era, until he was exposed as a fraud and killed himself.

Who did what, to whom, and to what effect, is the

story of this book, though so lost in myth and legend, and in the wreaths of ganja smoke are many of the events that it's an unreliable history at best. When the facts seem to diverge most, I've tried to retain the participant's own words so that the reader can make up his or her own mind as to what is the authorized version, but this is a difficult undertaking and there's no easy guarantee of truth (the first casualty of war). They came, they spliffed, they conquered, and then they fell out, would seem to be the moral of the tale. But there's a fair bit of entertainment along the way.

A SENSE OF PLACE

A Friday night in May 1996: cider-charged kiddies race their Escorts around the convenient circuit of the centre; others stumble by foot over the grass verges of what was once part of the harbour to Ritzy's, the big leisure-industry club where tonight Sapphire, a legendary Bristol nightlife character who cross- dresses as a woman, is hosting an alternative house night with Jon of the Pleased Wimmin as the star DJ. Minicabs lie in wait for illicit fares and drunken gangs crowd around the fast-food stands and late-night cafes, gorging on hot dogs and beefburgers. Glasses are broken underfoot and people are being sick. All in all, it's not what you'd call a laid-back, spliffed-up scene, and surprisingly, everything seems to move at normal speed ...

Over the road by the dockside, the city is celebrating the Festival of the Sea to commemorate the five-hundredth anniversary of John Cabot's voyage to Newfoundland. Organized by the city council, the festival costs twenty pounds a ticket and thoroughfares have been closed off to enforce the toll. The event has caused some controversy locally as it omits to mention the slave trade, the principal cause of Bristol's mercantile wealth in the eighteenth century, as well as locking out its citizens from the docks for a weekend. On a BBC One television programme about the festivities the three members of Massive Attack have been interviewed sitting on the steps of the Colston Hall (named after a famous Bristol merchant and slaver), complaining about the fact that the festival, and Bristol generally, doesn't acknowledge its slave heritage.

Shipshape and Bristol Fashion

Bristol is a difficult city to read and it takes some time to get beyond the rather bland surface it presents to outsiders. It doesn't have the aggressive urban culture of Liverpool (its main rival as a slave port in the eighteenth century) Newcastle or Manchester, and despite having a population of close to half a million, it tends to be perceived by visiting football fans as a kind of honorary village, the supporters of its two chronically unsuccessful football teams taunted as sheep shaggers and country yokels.

One local guidebook suggests that a possible crest for the city could feature a hand with two fingers raised in the direction of London and the rest of the country. Certainly it's a place that doesn't much care what people think of it. 'In Bath they live in fine houses and are poor, in Bristol shabby ones and are rich', reported the writer Charles Dibdin in 1797. Until the Industrial Revolution it was England's second city and this eminence has bred a sense of complacency second to none. With all of its natural advantages and its unparalleled setting by the Avon gorge, ringed with hills and watered by the Avon and the Frome, the city could have been another Rome, the same guidebook reports, but simply couldn't be bothered.

The local dialect sounds rather countrifed to outsiders, the soft West Country burr suggesting Somerset or Devon, though on closer listening it has a much harder edge and varies greatly between its different constituencies; there's South-Bristolian and North-Bristolian dialects; West-Indian Bristolian; posh Bristolian, even trustafarian-trying-to-be-streetwise Bristolian. The city is relatively compact; it's not part of a big conurbation and the suburbs soon give way to open countryside. Even from the toughest city, council estates like Southmead, Hartcliffe or Knowle West, the green hills of the Cotswolds or the Mendips remain in plain sight.

The Bristol Scene

One of the by-products of the success of the Bristol sound is that the city has been visited by countless journalists on a mission to find the happening scene that must have given rise to the music, and every major newspaper and magazine has run its 'User's Guide to Bristol' feature. The catalogue of clubs, clothes-and-record stores and bars that results tends to be very like those in similar guides to Nottingham, Sheffield or anywhere else on the continuum of style-journalists' interests ('Yes, they do have coffee!'), that tends to make everywhere outside of London into a hicksville version of Old Compton Street. Needless to say, the notion of a Bristol-sound scene doesn't really exist. Yes, you can see Massive's Robert Del Naja playing football on the downs of a Sunday or drinking in a bar; Daddy G and Mushroom often DJ in the local clubs; Portishead, Massive and Smith and Mighty have studios here; but it's hardly a trip-hop version of the Bloomsbury group, with the participants living in and out of each other's pockets.

It's a cause of some local acrimony that the Bristol bands don't actually perform in Bristol. Portishead have played one gig, at the New Trinity Centre in 1995, though as the event was advertised wrongly as lasting till 2a.m. and they actually went on stage at 9p.m., many people arrived to find them already finished. Massive held a sound-system party at the city's Ashton Court mansion in early 1995, which was wildly oversubscribed (it is said that it was overbooked on the strength of the guest list alone) and a Christmas 1995 party at New Trinity, but they have yet to play as a band, as they have done elsewhere in Europe. There is no Bristol-sound salon, though it's an intriguing thought, and Tricky has become a lost boy, rarely visiting the city of his illustrious birth. One day perhaps, there'll be a statue of him on the centre, cradling a spliff and looking out over the docks towards America, like the bronze effigy of John Cabot ...

Unlike other cities of its size, there are few civic initiatives for the arts, no tradition of festivals (until the Festival of the Sea) other than the unofficial Bristol Community Festival at Ashton Court, which is Europe's biggest free festival, and, perhaps, little sense that the culture of the city is the business of the people who live there. One of the most famous artists in the world, Richard Long, is a Bristolian and he lives here still, though there's no real recognition of the fact. The Theatre Royal is one of the oldest working theatres in the country but it's continually on the verge of financial ruin. In the mid- sixties, it was briefly at the centre of the city's only real golden age in the arts (pre hip-hop at least) when Peter O'Toole was in rep, plays were written by Peter Nichols and Peter Barnes, and Tom Stoppard wrote about them in the *Western Daily Press*.

Although the Arnolfini gallery on the harbour side is one of Europe's leading centres for contemporary art, it is funded almost wholly by the Arts Council and receives very little local money (though many locals would grudge it any at all). For years the ruling Labour group on the city council has shown a distrust of what it sees as elitist culture, and has tended to fund community arts projects rather than the city's own theatre or art galleries. Some city council-backed initiatives, like the Basement Music Workshop at Sefton Park Youth Club in St Andrews, have made an impact on the Bristol-sound scene, training up disaffected youngsters in the arts of drum and bass.

The traditional industries - tobacco, chocolate, sherry ('call them industries?', you can imagine a harsh northern voice protesting) and aerospace, are mostly in decline and long ago the city docks moved out to the container port of Avonmouth, just across the river from Portishead. But a measure of prosperity – and Bristol takes great pride in being a prosperous city – has continued through the growth of a financial services sector. New cultural industries based around broadcasting – the BBC has studios here – and animation (it's the home of Aardman studios, whose famous director Nick Park has won three Oscars) have also been established, and Bristol is a major media city of sorts, though in a typically unassuming way.

In the war the old city centre was badly bombed and a new shopping centre, Broadmead, was put up in its place – a grey, unloved, concrete jungle of chain stores, patrolled by young mums pushing buggies, kids from the outlying estates hanging out, and winos, beggars and crusties colonizing the underpass that separates the centre from the A38 main road opposite. As a staging post on the West-Country-festival circuit of the summer, Bristol has become a city of beggars for much of the year, with crusty punks and hippies mingling with sad, care-in-the-community inadequates in shop doorways and on street corners. Many of the crusty beggars are junkies and there's a strong trade in heroin which affects even the outlying estates.

When people talk about the prettiness of Bristol and its architectural splendours they usually mean Clifton, a large suburb of grand Georgian houses and Victorian crescents begun in the late eighteenth century on the top of the Avon gorge, when the river-side atmosphere of neighbouring Hotwells down below became too poisonous to sustain the good health its spa waters had previously promoted. Elsewhere, the good buildings, such as those in the business district just off the centre, are pinched in between brutalist tower blocks and toyshop post-modern offices, home to building societies or in-surance companies. It's been suggested that Bristolians have traditionally been willing to destroy the past because of a supreme confidence in the prosperity of the present and its inevitable continuance into the future, each generation content to provide its own monuments for posterity.

Despite the vandalism of the past, enough remains to make the city seem, on a good day, a very congenial kind of place.The waterside views of the floating harbour, the decayed terraces of Clifton and even the funky, distressed inner-city character of Montpelier look pretty enough, and in the sunshine the local Bath stone shimmers with a golden glow. At such times, lazing around takes on something of the air of a moral duty and it's then that Bristol's reputation as a laid- back city comes into its own, a quirk of civic character that may well lend itself to the music the city produces. The hills on which the city is built have encouraged generations of skateboarders and mountain bikers and perhaps helped to promote the necessary prerequisites for a slacker's lifestyle. Kids in Bristol don't usually aspire to moving on, and visiting students get stranded here quite happily, forming a substantial rump of graduates who never found their way back home.

Round and About

The surface of the city is riven by chasms and full of holes. From the deep fissure of the Avon Gorge through which the river bends its way into the port, the high Gothic cliffs spanned by Brunel's famous suspension bridge (where local suicides still go to end themselves), to the New Cut and Floating Harbour which were built to make the port navigable as far as the city centre, the skin of the city has been cut and peeled. A network of underground waterways lies beneath the centre, and old mining tunnels criss- cross the entire city, sometimes resulting in sudden subsidence in the houses built above them. At Goldney

House in Clifton, there's a famous underground grotto, lined with seashells, and built for the habitation of a picturesque hermit, and there are caves all over the place, including an underground chamber by St Mary Redcliffe Church which was rumoured, wrongly, to be a place where slaves were held in chains. Just beneath the suspension bridge on Hotwell Road is the blocked-up entrance to the Clifton-Hotwells Railway, a white-elephant enterprise built at the turn of the century to connect the two suburbs, with a tunnel burrowed heroically through the rock, but shortly afterwards abandoned. During the war it was commandeered by the BBC for use as a secret bomb-proof broadcasting station and storeroom.

In Bristol, you continually go up and down hills as you move from one neighbourhood to another and each ascent or descent has a social and economic, as well as a topographic, significance, for the city is neatly demarcated by contour lines indicating relative wealth or poverty. North of the river, the uptown suburbs tumble down the incline of prosperity, from posh Clifton to well-to-do Redland, Cotham and Kingsdown until they meet the social divide of the A38, the Cheltenham or Gloucester road. Then come the in-betweenies of Bishopston, St Andrews and Montpelier, where the inner city begins. A neat social division invented by the residents or their estate agents separates bohemian Montpelier into upper or lower sectors, the lower shading off into St Paul's, which represents, in estate-agents' terms, that bourne from which no house seeker returns. Cruelly stigmatized by Bristolians because of its relatively high proportion of non-white residents, and its reputation for crime, drugs and prostitution, St Paul's is an area with few amenities, constantly trawled by police cars and vans seeking revenge for the hiding they received in the 1980 St Paul's riot. Its front line is, compared to say Brixton, pathetically small: a few pubs and cafes, a scattering of shops including Nubian Records, a sports shop and travel agent (Caribbean flights a speciality) and the St Paul's advice centre. Old Jamaican men sit outside the betting shop on sunny days and taxi drivers hang around their office, waiting for calls. Young girls in unfeasibly short skirts stand by the telephone boxes on City Road as the lines of cars pass along the road. At night the drivers pass very slowly.

St Paul's is also a place for music and entertainment and many of Bristol's leading clubs are based on the edge of the district, like Lakota, which used to be the Moon Club, and Club Loco, which used to be the Tropic, and the Blue Mountain. These clubs, which are owned and operated by Bristolian West Indians, have traditionally been the hipper, more alternative venues where there is the most interplay between black and white, in contrast to the big leisure-industry clubs of the centre, which are dominated by white kids from the suburbs and estates. At weekends the clubs are invaded by outsiders, particularly the Welsh from across the Severn bridge, and Bristol has built up the reputation of a happening night-time city, with licensing laws extending club opening hours to 6a.m. or later.

Across the M32 motorway is Easton, a sprawling suburb that is home to far more black residents than St Paul's, with significantly more schools and amenities, and the beginnings of a music industry in Unit 23 of the Easton Business Centre, which is home to Roni Size's Full Cycle label, the leading drum and bass imprint. From the Asian clothing factories and late-opening grocers of Stapleton road, Easton begins to go uphill once again, out of the inner city into the rather characterless suburbs of St George and Fishponds which lead out towards Bath or the northern-motorway network. South of the river the pattern is almost reversed, as the gentrified housing of Southville goes uphill into working-class Bedminster, Totterdown, Knowle, Withywood and Hartcliffe, before the rise of the Mendips signals the start of the commuter villages of the countryside.

Slavery

What does strike a stranger to Bristol are some of the street names: Whiteladies Road, Blackboy Hill, Jamaica Street. Like much of the grander architecture – the palatial Clifton houses now converted into flats, the almshouses, schools and municipal hall named after the merchant Edward Colston, and his statue – these names are a testimony to the impact the slave trade has had on the city (though it's said that Whiteladies Road and Blackboy Hill pre-date any involvement with slavery), and the incredible wealth both it and the sugar plantations the slaves worked on, brought home. Everyone in Bristol is aware of this heritage. There's a kind of secret underground knowledge about the trade – like the rumours of caves under St Mary Redcliffe where slaves are supposed to have been manacled – which often isn't knowledge at all, but folk tales, conspiracy theories, fantasies. Nevertheless, there exists a general consensus about Bristol's shady past and its sense of guilt, and those without much share in the city's wealth take great delight or anger in remembering where so much of it came from.

The relevance of all this to the Bristol sound is obvious: black music, made by people of African descent, with Caribbean and mixed-race roots, in a city where many of the major monuments and street names recall the slave trade, inevitably reflects some of that heritage, whether consciously or not. Without wishing to suggest that slavery and the music are connected in any vulgar Bristol fashion, the heritage does mean that questions of race inevitably carry a strong historical resonance. For the Festival of the Sea, a replica of Cabot's ship, the *Matthew*, was built on a platform just below St Mary Redcliffe (the first Queen Elizabeth's favourite church), where the corporation ordered the bells to be rung after one of Wilberforce's abolition motions had been turned down by parliament, and within a few feet of those sinister caves. When the ship was completed and a ceremony was held to celebrate its launch, local dignitaries in tuxedos were confronted by protestors who wanted attention focused on the city's role in the slave trade instead. Many of the dignitaries were members of the Society for Merchant Venturers, a rather secretive organization that once functioned as a slavers' pressure group, and continues to represent some of the most powerful interests in the city. Of course, they do a lot of work for charity.

The symbolic resonance provided by Bristol's role in the slave trade is also difficult to ignore. The famous triangular route linked the city with Africa, where, usually on the Guinea coast, trinkets and sometimes guns and gin were exchanged for slaves; then on to the West Indies or the American colonies, where the slaves were sold and a cargo of produce brought back home, with a profit made on each leg of the journey if the captain was lucky. Thus each of what were to become the great cultures of popular music flowed in and out of the ships of Bristol merchants. When, after the 1952 McCarran-Walter Act banned the migration of West Indians to the United States, and the descendants of West-Indian slaves started to come to Britain, the trade flowed back to Bristol at last.

The beginnings of the slave trade in Bristol pre-date Cabot's great voyage by a number of years. In 1552 Captain Thomas Wyndham sailed from Kingroad on the Avon to the Barbary Coast in command of three well-laden merchant ships, and four years later the pirate Hawkins carried his first load of Africans to the West Indies. Until the Restoration in 1660 the trade was largely unregulated and widely disapproved of, and also centred in London, whose monopolies had led Bristol to favour the parliamentary side in the Civil War (although, typically, the city hedged its bets). After Restoration, the Company of Royal Adventurers of England Trading into Africa – the Royal Africa

Company – was formed, with a charter that specifically mentioned slaving as one of its objects. At first Bristol merchants were shut out of the trade, but Edward Colston moved to London and eventually became a member of the Royal Africa Company, breaking into the clique of city slickers. By 1698 the monopoly was broken and the great days of the Bristol slave trade began.

By 1709, fifty-seven ships from Bristol were engaged in the trade, which the Corporation of Bristol and the Society of Merchant Venturers called, in a neat little civic slogan, 'the great support of our people at home, and the foundation of our trade abroad'. In the 1750s, Bristol may have surpassed London to become the leading slave port (though it was soon overtaken by Liverpool), and there were 155 merchants trading in slaves. A number of ancillary industries grew up to support the trade; the production of iron, brass and woollen goods for trading in Africa; a trade with the fisheries of Labrador in order to meet the needs of the slaves' diet, and insurance for the vessels and their cargo (slaves were insured at five shillings a head), though it was established that slaves dying from jumping overboard and swallowing salt water were not the responsibility of the underwriters. Almost the whole local population was involved in the trade in some way, and according to the anti-slavery campaigner Thomas Clarkson, 'Everyone seemed to execrate it, but no one thought of its abolition.'

From 1698 to 1807 it's estimated that between seven and ten million African slaves were forcibly carried across the Atlantic by English ships; in 1788 alone there were 74,000. In 1737 Read's *Journal of London* published an extract of a letter from the Bristol ship *Princess of Orange*, stating that on the way to the West Indies, 'A hundred of the men slaves jumped overboard, and it was with great difficulty that we saved as many as we did. We lost 33 who were resolved to die. Some others have died since but not

to the owner's loss, they being sold before any dis-
covery was made of the injury the salt water had done
to them. The captain has lost two of his own slaves.'

Interestingly, musicians were employed on some
slaving ships; in August 1729 the *Castle of Bristol* had
a piper, a fiddler and a drummer on board. Captains
were also allowed to transport a few slaves for their
personal profit and because of this tradition slaves
were brought back to Bristol to work as servants,
where they sometimes escaped and occasionally
survived to become free men. The *Bristol Journal* of
March 12th, 1757 advertised the 'elopement' of a
young negro called Starling, 'who blows the French
horn very well', and some of the runaway slaves are
described as wearing silver collars around the neck,
engraved with their master's name. In 1768 a Captain
Read announced in the *Bristol Journal* that he had not
murdered his negro servant, 'whatever people may
say'.

The trade also took its toll on the crews. Out of 940
men who made up the crews of 24 Bristol slavers in
1787, 216 died during the voyage, 239 deserted or
were discharged in the plantations, 10 out of 56
completed the voyage in one vessel, and 14 out of 44
in another. It was the plight of the seamen rather than
the slaves that was the main spur in the move towards
abolition. Clarkson found that more seamen died 'in
three slave vessels in a given time than in all the other
Bristol vessels put together, numerous as they were'.

As the inevitability of abolition approached, and
with Liverpool having long ago overtaken Bristol as a
slave port, the merchants took their money out of
slaving and put it into West–Indian estates, continuing to prosper from the consequences of the trade.
The city also did very well out of compensation once
abolition had occurred, campaigning vigorously for a
fair settlement of their losses.

Though all this may seem a very long time ago, you
can still sit in the city's Commercial Rooms in the

business district, built as a club for the merchants around 1800, and now a rather tawdry theme pub, and watch the clock face on the wall which, connected to a weather vane on the roof, tells which way the wind is blowing. A strong westerly breeze used to get the merchants excited – large ones all round, no doubt – as they knew their ships were on their way home from the plantations and that a profit would soon be turned.

St Paul's

Much later, after the Second World War, St Paul's became the destination for a number of West Indians who had served in the RAF and thereafter took up residence in Bristol. In the early sixties, after a number of Caribbean immigrants had made the city their home, Bristol became the site of one of the major incidents in British post-war race relations, when a strike at the Bristol Omnibus Company developed after the majority of white bus drivers and conductors voted to protest about non-whites being employed there. A spirited defence was mounted and the leader of the opposition, Harold Wilson, visited the city and compared the boycott, which was backed by the company, to apartheid in South Africa. At length, the company was forced to back down.

A remarkable participant-observer sociological study of St Paul's, *Endless Pressure*, by a black Jamaican academic, Ken Pryce, was published in 1979, just before the riot, and it paints a vivid picture of life in the area. 'The community of West Indians in Bristol is made up almost entirely of working-class Jamaicans,' Pryce reports. 'They are predominantly country people and a high proportion of them hail from the parish of St Thomas in Jamaica.' Pryce categorizes the West Indian inhabitants of St Paul's, or 'Shanty Town', as he sometimes calls it, into five groups: hustlers, teeny-

(ABOVE AND OPPOSITE) A blues dance in St Paul's in the early eighties.
According to sociologist Ken Pryce, 'an institution for sinners, representing a
kind of profane, grass-roots, secularity among shanty-town West Indians.'
(*photos:* Mike Norris)

boppers, proletarian respectables, the saved, and the
in-betweeners, though the essential distinction he
makes is between 'those who work and those who
hustle'. For his research, Pryce hangs out on the front
line, goes to clubs and blues dances and smokes dope,
but he also goes to church and actually gets baptized.

'For the stable law-abiding West Indians who still live there', he writes, 'St Paul's is regarded as a low-status area to be moved out of as quickly as possible ... In the shops and on the pavements West Indians, Pakistanis, Indians, Poles and the Irish, mix freely with a wide range of deviant and disreputable types seeking escape from the burdens of failure in the wider social world.'

Pryce, you feel after reading his book, is a serious man, as near to 'the saved' as to the 'expressive-disreputable orientation' he favours in his research. He befriends a hustler and pimp, Strode, and watches as he controls his women and defends his ground at the 'Plantation Club', the after-hours joint the hustlers favour. He notes the growing influence of Rastafarianism and militant reggae, and its attraction for the teeny-boppers, and 'their psychic disorientation and confusion in the face of hostility and rejection and their growing alienation from white society'. The blues dance, he says, 'is an institution for sinners, representing a kind of profane, grassroots secularity among Shanty-Town West Indians.' The research finshed and the book published, Pryce left for a teaching job at the University of Trinidad. Shortly afterwards, in April 1980, the teeny-boppers had their revenge, when St Paul's exploded into a full-scale riot, the first and the most significant of the many subsequent revolts of the Thatcher years.

The Riot

In the folklore of Bristol, and of Bristol music especially, St Paul's has a significance out of all proportion to its size. For a white man to move freely about St Paul's, going to the blues, hanging out with the hustlers, is to be the equivalent of Norman Mailer's white Negro, or Jack Kerouac's hipster, who 'at lilac evening walked with every muscle aching amongst the lights of 27th and Welton in the Denver coloured section, wishing I were a Negro, feeling that the best the white world offered was not enough ecstasy for me, not enough life, joy, kicks, darkness, music, not enough night'. A notable feature of the riot was that a number of white people were involved, many of them punks who lived there, taking advantage of the cheap, rented accommodation in the area, as many people still do today, hanging out on the greens between the housing blocks, smoking dope and drinking cans of beer, and watching the events unfold.

Paul Johnson, the brother of Miles Johnson from the Wild Bunch, and himself associated with the Wild-Bunch crew, remembers sitting on the green having a smoke and watching the police being repelled from the Black and White Café, which they had raided in search of drugs and illegal alcohol. At 3.30p.m. on April 2nd, 1980, twenty police officers raided the café on Grosvenor Road with a warrant to search for drugs. As the police were unloading crates of alcohol from the café into their van a flashpoint occurred, possibly the famous case of the torn trouser suffered by a black social worker, Dr Prince Brown, which received much publicity later on (Brown, watching the police leave the café, claimed that in the mêlée one of them had torn his trousers, and was justifiably upset). Whatever the cause, the police were attacked and stoned and forced to take cover in the café, and attacked again when they made a run for their vehicles. Johnson remembers someone making a petrol bomb and throwing it at an empty, overturned police car, after which he retired from the fray, returning only later that night, when the area was in full riot, the police having withdrawn from 7.30p.m. to 11.30p.m., and wondering if he was part of the cause of it all.

Situated in Grosvenor Road, which was stigmatized by Pryce as symbolising 'everything that is most profane in the world of coloured people', the Black and White Café was undeniably a place where drugs – or at least cannabis – were sold. It had been raided at least three times before, but without any serious trouble. While the twenty policemen entered the café that day, many more officers were placed outside, including members of the Division 'A' Task Force, a West-Country version of London's Special Patrol Group. The officers entered the café, snatched cigarettes from people's mouths and questioned those present, refusing to allow anyone to leave without revealing their names and addresses. Bertram Wilkes, the owner of the café, was arrested and led away in handcuffs, in full view of the angry crowd waiting outside.

When officers emerged carrying the booty of illegal drugs and alcohol, it is said that a cry went up from the people outside of 'They've got the drugs!' and the riot proper began. Between 4p.m. and 7p.m. there were a series of running battles between the police – armed with truncheons and dustbin lids – and gangs of black and white youths throwing stones, bricks and bottles. Although it was later estimated that the police had miscalculated by timing their raid on the day the school holidays had begun, when disaffected youngsters were therefore able to contribute to the mêlée, a number of the ordinary residents of the district also got involved. At the trial which followed, a PC Sherman recalled cowering behind a wall, hopping on an injured foot, when a sixty–year–old white woman pushed him out of his hiding place, shouting 'Go out there and get yourself killed, you white bastard!'

After the police withdrew, widespread looting took place. When, late at night, they moved back in, supported by officers from all over the West Country, the whole commercial centre of St Paul's had been trashed. In the course of the riot, fifty policemen were injured, twenty-two of whom required hospital treatment. Eleven civilians were also hospitalised and twenty-five police vehicles were damaged at an estimated cost of £40,000, six of them burned beyond repair. Twenty-one buildings were damaged or burnt out, including a bank and a post office, at a cost of £300,000. The activities of the looters cost a further £150,000.

The photographer Beezer (Andy Beese) remembers walking down Stoke's Croft at the edge of St Paul's, 'going to buy some weed, when somebody said there's a riot going on. In a big shock we found ourselves in the middle of the riot, with people looting the shops. Everyone got involved, there were all kinds of people there and all the junkies were standing outside the chemist's trying to get the crowd to loot it, but no one was interested, they wanted to get hold of like, linen or whatever from the proper shops. We bundled up some cigarettes and stashed them in my flat.' Mark

Stewart, who was at home that day and didn't know what was going on, remembers getting phone calls from mates in phone boxes saying things like 'We've got the fags, we're going to get the motorbikes shortly.' Sapphire remembers the riot as 'quite fun, almost amusing. I was walking down the road when I saw a man running past carrying a television that he had looted from somewhere. He dropped the aerial and I caught up with him and gave it to him, telling him the telly wouldn't be much use without it.'

Over a hundred people were charged with criminal offences arising from the riot and sixteen people were eventually selected for the charge of riotous assembly, an offence second only to treason, with a penalty of up-to-life imprisonment. Jimmy Walsh, one of only two white youths involved in the case, fitted the description of 'a punk' seen looting a betting shop, and he was known to the police as someone who 'ran' with the Mighty brothers, Clifton and Raymond. The case against Clive Edwards, another defendant, was dropped when evidence was heard that the police officer who chased him called him Raymond Mighty. The case against Walsh was also dismissed. Four officers mentioned Clifton Mighty in their statements, one saying he saw him throwing stones at the Black and White Café, but he was found not guilty. His brother Raymond - later of Smith and Mighty - disappeared from St Paul's after the riot and was never brought to trial.

The consequences of the riot were many and, for a while, the attention of the whole country was concentrated on St Paul's. The complete infrastructure of the area had been demolished, banks and shops destroyed, buildings fired, the forces of law and order pushed out of the area until what remained was a blazing wreck. Tensions between black immigrants and the police had become so extreme that a real, US-style riot had ensued, and society at large was appalled. Within a year subsequent riots in London, Birmingham

and many other cities would occur and the events of
St Paul's would begin to seem symptomatic of a
wider malaise, of protests against the Thatcher years.
But Bristol was where it started and the reputation
of St Paul's as the toughest of the tough had been
established.

FROM PUNK TO THE WILD BUNCH

Trying to find reasons for the sudden growth of a new musical culture in Bristol is a difficult business. You could, admittedly, draw a line between Acker Bilk (from nearby Pensford), Adge Cutler and the Wurzels and Massive Attack or Tricky, but it would be a very blurred one. The move from cider to spliff as the drug of choice would also have to be accommodated, though Massive have met the Wurzels and talk admiringly of their alleged appetite for stimulants in the old days. There's not even an equivalent to Liverpool's beat boom to bridge the gap; the Avon must have been the only major river in Britain not to have a sound named after it and, as noted earlier, Russ Conway was probably the last Bristolian prior to Massive Attack to see any sustained chart action.

The development of the Bristol sound is perhaps more than anything part of the worldwide change in musical culture brought about by hip-hop and parallel innovations in music technology, replacing the gig with the club or party jam, and the familiar instruments of guitar, drum and bass with turntables, samplers and the midi interface; even replacing the traditional figure of the musician with the DJ or mixer and his essential counterpart, the clued-up engineer such as Portishead's Dave McDonald. But that doesn't explain the peculiar character of Bristol hip-hop, its slowness, its emphasis on songs, its echoes of reggae and soul. There are strong links to be traced between what preceded the arrival of sound-system crews cutting up break beats, and the social and musical roots of the crews themselves, which pre-dated hip-hop by a number of years. The very way those break beats were manipulated, and what made them so distinctive, was related directly to the city's musical heritage in punk and reggae, especially the slow burn of lover's rock. The members of the Wild Bunch, Massive Attack (excepting the younger Mushroom), and Smith and Mighty were all punks for a time, and Tricky was a two-tone rude boy. They would attend concerts by visiting punk acts at the Berkeley Rooms or the Top Rank and gather with others of their tribe, looking ostentatiously disaffected, outside Virgin records in Broadmead. Much of the ideological baggage of punk, has, therefore, along with the rhythmic base of reggae, continued to affect the music and attitudes of the Bristol-sound bands.

Punk and Reggae

The pre-hip-hop scene in the early eighties in Bristol was notable for a number of local reggae bands. The St Paul's-based Black Roots was an act with an international reputation, an Avon equivalent of Steel Pulse, who toured abroad as much as at home. Other, racially-mixed bands, like Talisman and Restriction (who featured Rob Smith of Smith and Mighty, with Portishead's Dave McDonald as their soundman), were popular attractions at local venues such as the Green Rooms or the Dockside Settlement. Visiting reggae stars like Gregory Isaacs or Dennis Brown would play the local Top Rank suite as part of national tours presented by black promoters, and Bristol-based reggae sound systems would work the circuit of black community centres in Gloucester, Birmingham, Wolverhampton, Swindon, Reading and London, while their counterparts in those cities would also visit

Bristol, where at St Paul's carnival time in the summer they would engage in sound-system clashes.

The underground of unlicensed blues dances in St Paul's also acted as a space for local sound systems, and the record shop Revolver – where Massive's Grant Marshall worked for a time – was a reliable repository of the latest reggae releases, its location in Clifton making it easy for white boys to browse without feeling intimidated. At one point in the late eighties, the famous ska and reggae trombonist Vin Gordon relocated to Bristol and formed a band, the Authentics, before the immigration authorities forced him to leave the country.

City Limits

In trying to assess the roots of the Bristol sound there's also the matter of the city of Bristol itself. Though it's rather far-fetched to try and draw a parallel between Bristol in the eighties with New Orleans' Storyville at the turn of the century, Chicago during Prohibition, Kansas City in the thirties, or Beale Steet in Memphis in the fifties, it's worth having a go, just for the hell of it. While there's little evidence for the interregnum of civic graft, sleaze and the consequent laissez-faire attitude to clubs and bordellos that the American examples suggest is a necessary pre-requisite to new musical movements, you could build a theory of sorts around the effects on the city of the shock waves emanating from the St Paul's riot of 1980.

The police had been given a good hiding and although they were not slow to exact reprisals – for a while St Paul's at night resembled a city under forced curfew, with police vans placed strategically in wait at the borders of the area in case further trouble occurred, or simply as a powerful symbolic warning as to who was ultimately in charge – a softly-softly approach was meant to be in operation. Some people felt that St

Paul's had become a no-go area, with the police under instructions to avoid possibly inflammatory raids, such as the one on the Black and White Café that had started the riot. Young black men in Bristol, many of whom used to get hassled by the police if they were caught hanging around in the centre, may also have become less likely targets for harassment in the wake of the riot, at least for a time, and therefore able to move more freely about the city.

Activities within St Paul's itself were also less liable to disruption by the police for a while, and the development of what was known as the Three Stripe Posse, out of which the producers Smith and Mighty emerged (themselves the first of the Bristol-sound artists to get a national reputation), began (or so it is said by their contemporaries) as a St Paul's-based street gang whose activities allegedly financed the purchase of the equipment to first start up a sound system and then begin recording. And while Bristol didn't have a wide open nightlife culture to rival New Orleans or Kansas City, it did have one club, the Dug Out, where black and white mixed fairly freely, unusual in a city centre where straight clubs like Romeo and Juliets used to operate an unofficial quota system in allowing entry to black men. And whatever the theory, the Dug Out really does play a big part in the story. It also links together the mini-boom that Bristol's musical culture did experience, in the post-punk bohemian fringe of the Pop Group, Pigbag and Rip Rig and Panic in the early eighties, with the sound-system crew that went on to become the basis of the Bristol sound, the legendary Wild Bunch.

The Dug Out

The Dug Out is remembered fondly by everyone who went there and since its enforced closure Bristol has never found another venue to replace it, though for a while the scene moved on to the Moon Club on the edge of St Paul's. Indeed, its reputation has reached quite mythic proportions, its role in the story of the Bristol sound becoming comparable to that of Minton's Playhouse and the clubs of 52nd Street in the history of bebop. Of course, like its historical forbears, it was also a dive, and it operated as a jazz club long before it became associated with hip-hop, with Bristolian jazz musicians like Keith Tippett and Larry Stabbins (of Working Week) paying their dues there by sitting in with the resident trad and mainstream bands while they were still at school in the mid-sixties.

Located on the site of what is now a Thai restaurant, in Park Row, just across the road from the university at the north-eastern edge of Clifton, the Dug Out lasted until 1986, when the police and the Park Street Trader's Association got it closed down after a number of violent incidents in the vicinity. During its high point in the eighties it was less a discotheque – its nominal function – than a rather gloriously dingy hang-out, a rabbit warren of inter-connecting cellar rooms that gradually grew to include a video lounge and a second clubroom upstairs, called, of course, 'Upstairs'. Everyone remembers the carpet, which would stick to your feet like some particularly viscous oil-based material, the fibres trying to follow you as you moved. Significantly, as noted, it was a place where downtown and uptown mixed, an almost unique space within the carefully-patrolled and segmented city where black kids from St Paul's and the estates met Clifton trendies and those from the white working-class tower blocks of Barton Hill and the outlying districts. Whether they actually did mix much is a disputed point to be returned to later, but at least the possibility of social miscegenation was there, even if it might not go much farther than a white boy or girl buying a 'quid twist' of grass from the black man who stood on the stairs.

'For me the Dug Out was like a legendary hang-out

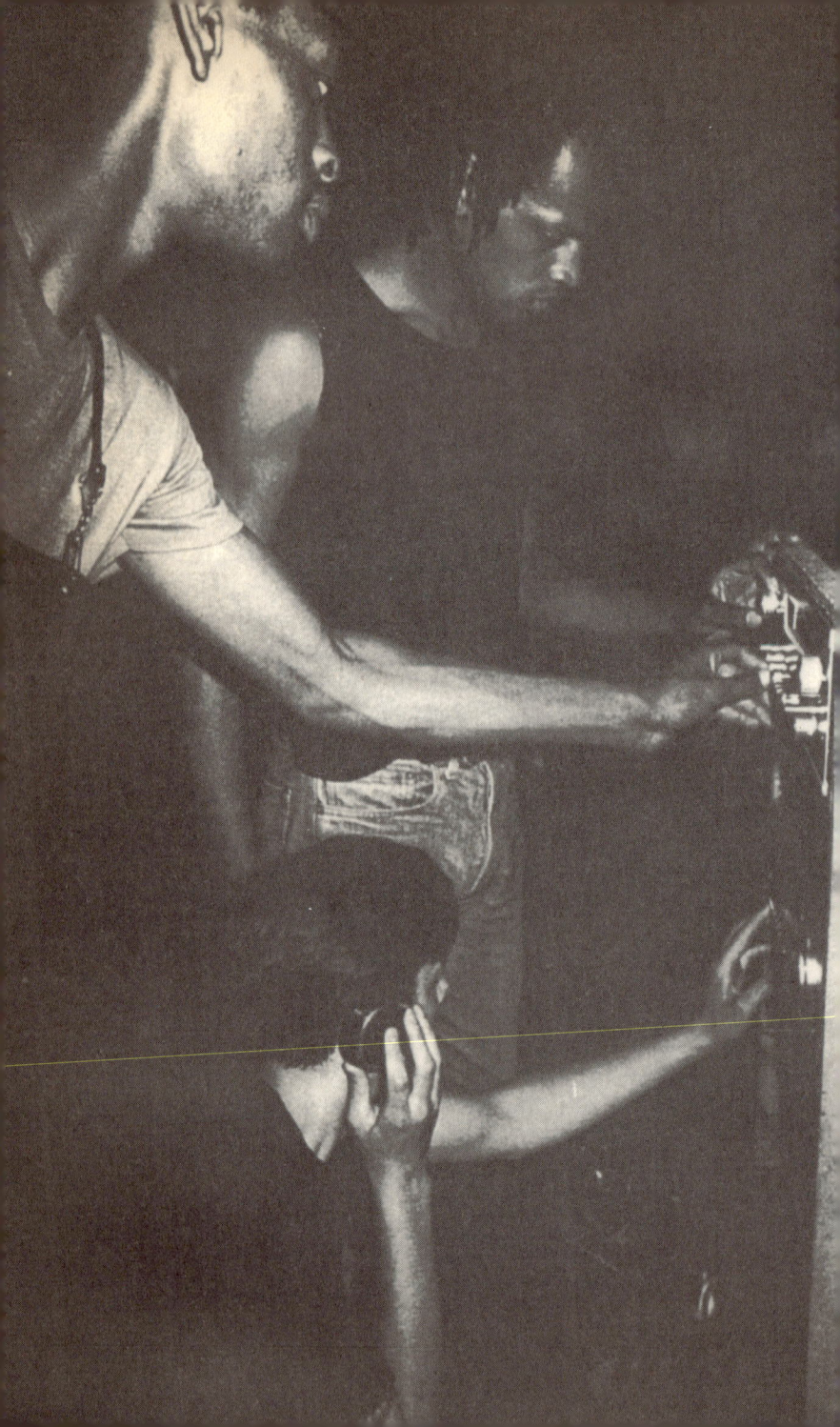

which was almost dangerous and exotic', remembers Massive's Robert Del Naja, who was introduced to the other members of the Wild Bunch there as a young punk into the Clash and reggae in the early eighties. 'Everyone talked about the danger and the trouble there and the history of it being a jazz club in the sixties. Suddenly it was like everyone was saying "Let's go down there and have a look". You'd go drinking in Clifton or Montpelier and then go down the Dug Out, and it became an every-day-of-the-week thing, the sort of club you'd go to Monday to Saturday. You'd do whatever you did in the day and then, like about eight-thirty go down the Dug Out, sit in the video room and watch a movie and then, by the time you turned round it was eleven-thirty and you were ready for a night out till two in the morning.

'What made the Dug Out good was that it was a place where you could chat, drink and communicate and get into the music. Nowadays you go out on a night till six in the morning and you're completely wiped out the next day, but in those days you could go out six nights a week, drinking Special Brew and smoking Red Leb, that was the combination. In terms of learning about the music the Dug Out for most people in Bristol was the only place you could mix. You had the pubs up in Clifton which was trendy, the Rip Rig and Panic, M4 sort of crowd, or down St Paul's at the blues, those were the two choices; or you were going to the Dug Out and mixing. That's why the Dug Out was such a threat, that's why it got closed down. I mean they blamed it on trouble and the rest of it but there was much more trouble going on down the centre, more fights, more stabbings, more shops being urinated on, shop windows being put through. It was more like the Dug Out brought the black people out of St Paul's into Clifton, and the traders – it was

(OPPOSITE) Grant, Nellee (kneeling) and Miles at the Dug Out in 1983 (*photo*: Beezer)

them who got it closed down – couldn't hack it at all.
And nor could the Old Bill because it meant things
weren't contained into one area and it freaked them
out, it was anarchy you know?'

'The Dug Out was the only place to go', remembers
the photographer Beezer, who took the pictures of the
Wild Bunch there in the early and mid-eighties, as the
group gradually came together after Grant Marshall
began working as the Dug Out's DJ in 1982. 'It was a
different crowd every night of the week and it was,
like, thirty pence to get in, maybe seventy-five at
weekends. I started going there in about 1977, when I
was thirteen. You had to lie about your age but no one
was really bothered. There were all kinds of scams.
Once, a local free sheet newspaper had advertised a
free drinks token for the club and we knew the person
who was delivering them so we nabbed the lot, about
five hundred copies, and kept presenting the tokens
for free drinks. Sometimes the barmaids would give
us a drink if we just pushed a button or five pence
over the counter until the manager found out and
banned us.'

'You'd walk in and immediately be confronted by
Max, the doorman, who used to just sit there and look
you up and down', remembers Oli Timmins, a designer
who produced artwork for the first Smith and Mighty
releases and who continues to collaborate with Robert
Del Naja. 'You'd show him your little membership card,
your passport to late-night drinking, and then you'd
walk down the stairs and end up in the middle of the
dance floor, where no one was dancing except maybe
Sapphire. You'd buy quid twists from the black guy
who stood on the stairs, little bits of paper with a few
bits of grass – always grass – mixed in, that you'd get
three or four spliffs from. There was always a fight.
Every night there would have to be a fight and it
would clear the place for a few minutes until someone
came and sorted it out. Sometimes people would let
off canisters of CS gas and everyone ran out.

'Everyone, absolutely everyone used to be there, and they'd be there every single night of the week. Because you paid a membership, it cost nothing or nearly nothing to get in, and the drinks were at pub prices and someone would always buy you a drink. It had an air of slight dodginess and it was a little bit scuzzy, which was good. Eventually, in the mid-eighties, the music started to come to the forefront, with 2 Bad Crew and Grant, and it started to change a bit and people began to dance, though not much. I remember being rather perturbed because I was into the Clash but I also liked disco music and they didn't seem to fit together, but then the Clash started to do disco-type things. Dub was really the saviour of it all, because it brought all the different things together.

'I'd go there when it opened and only just make it home after it closed. On the last week before it closed down they had free drinks from nine to ten o'clock and you'd go to the bar and order like ten tequilas. It wasn't like clubs today, no one frisked you on the way in, and you could go on your own and be sure of meeting someone that you knew. The owner, Brian Jones, was a great guy. He was into offshore powerboat racing and he sometimes used to park his boat outside the club. He obviously made so much money that he let people do what they wanted, as long as they were within reason. The atmosphere was a lot to do with the kids who went there, who tended to be the more street-aware kids, who didn't want to dress up for a disco but wanted to wear their ripped jeans, and because of that it did become a kind of melting pot with people from all over the city and where it didn't matter if you were black or white.'

Paul Johnson remembers it differently: 'At the Dug Out everyone who was someone was there, it was the place to go and be seen, but there was absolutely no conversation across the social boundaries and the melting pot thing is an illusion. People from different areas would go but they wouldn't get on. Nellee was

The Wild Bunch
at the Dug Out
in 1984.
Left to right:
Miles, Grant,
Nellee, Claude,
Delge.
(*photo*: Beezer)

there with the Clifton people – saying "ya" instead of yes, but I felt that they treated me like I was thick because I came from St Paul's. I didn't like the Clifton music anyway – Pigbag, Rip Rig and Panic and them – it was too trendy. I liked funk bass and heavy beats, like Parliament and Funkadelic.'

'I used to go to the Oasis, on the gay scene', remembers Sapphire, 'and one night I says to my friends, this is a bit boring, let's go down the Dug Out. "You're wearing a dress, you'll get beat up" they said, but I went in there and felt the vibe, got on the dance floor, cracked open my amyl nitrate and hoisted my dress over my head. You could do anything. To give you an idea of how free it was I used to pick guys off the dance floor and give them blow jobs in the toilets. One night I had two guys in the cubicle and the manager was standing right outside the door and he could see the tail of my coat on the floor. I wasn't bothered and just went out of there smiling, but the guys were a bit scared about coming out.

'I used to practically live there, it was my home and when it closed part of my life was gone, like taking off an arm. It was ahead of its time in terms of everything. In those days clubs were quite clichéd but in the Dug Out you had students, pimps, queens, decent folks, drop outs, a whole mixture of people there to have fun. People did mix, but it all depended who you were. I was black and gay and I would mix, but there would be groups of black guys who would just sit and smoke their spliffs, or stand around looking cool – if you spilled a drink on them they made you pay for the dry cleaning the next day. Even on a Monday night it was packed. People tell me that they would go because there were a lot of nurses and they were supposed to be easy and randy when they got drunk ... in the end there were too many young black kids from St Paul's selling drugs to all the white kiddies, and that gave the police a better chance to close it down.'

Marc Crewe, who was the rock editor of the local

Sapphire (right) and friend at the Dug Out in 1984. 'When it closed part of my life had gone, like taking off an arm.' (*photo*: Beezer)

listings magazine *Venue* throughout the period, says: 'The irony of the club was that really it should have been in St Paul's, not Clifton. It was the only place in the city where you got such a mixed crowd and the roots of what it became began in the punk days, when they even used to have punk bands playing live, who were always terrible, and they played reggae in the breaks, which all the punks as well as the rastas who went there were into. The police really used to hate it though, because it was letting the black kids into Clifton. I remember one night when there was a stabbing outside the club somewhere, which had nothing to do with the Dug Out, but about thirty police came in and rounded everyone up, getting

Wild Bunch (*photo:* Beezer)

them outside and searching them while the blood from the guy who had been stabbed was pouring down the gutters.'

Dug Out Music

When hip-hop took off in the early eighties, it didn't enter a vacuum (or at least it did so only for those listeners who were very young at the time), but rather it was received within the club culture of the Dug Out, and other venues like the Dockside Settlement in St

Paul's, into a scene where roots reggae, lover's rock and dub were already well-established, along with the late-punk sound of the Clash and the contemporary black music of soul and jazz-funk that any club would have been playing as an incentive to dancers. What began as the loose affiliation of the Wild Bunch had connections which substantially pre-dated the emergence of hip-hop, and their sound system reflected this, mixing reggae, funk and electro together quite naturally. Miles Johnson, Nellee Hooper, Paul Johnson and Rob Chant (later to play with Smith and Mighty) had already been in a post-punk band called Recluse Youth; Hooper had played percussion with another Pop Group boho-funk offshoot, Maximum Joy, and also with Pigbag, with whom he appeared on *Top of the Pops*. By the time Miles Johnson came back from a short spell in prison in 1982 (for which, so it's said, he took the rap for someone else) hip-hop had truly happened and the heroic era of the Wild Bunch began in earnest.

Boho Punk

The great days of the Dug Out were also just after the time when Bristol's musical culture had at last become self-confident and found a measure of success with a readily identifiable sound. After the city's low profile during the beat-boom and rock years, at least as regards national recognition, by the punk days of the late seventies things were starting to happen, with the emergence of the Pop Group, led by Mark Stewart, and the Cortinas, led by Jeremy Valentine. Later, there was the inevitable local compilation album, inevitably called *Avon Calling*, and the start of influential post-punk groups like the Brilliant Corners and the Blue Aeroplanes. There was also The *Bristol Recorder*, a series of record/magazine anthologies put out by a group who eventually ended up as the Womad-festival team now based at Peter Gabriel's Real World Studios near Bath. The first Womad festival, held in Shepton Mallet in 1982, was an inspired event which gathered together musicians from all over the world, including local boho punks Rip Rig and Panic. Though it lost a fortune (causing Gabriel to bail it out), it can be seen in retrospect as the high point of the tribal funk ethic to which so many of the bohemian Bristol bands of the era seemed to dedicate themselves.

At the end of the seventies and the beginning of the eighties a scene developed superintended by Pop Group manager and general animateur Dick O'Dell, with the Y record label, the Pop Group and their spin-off bands Pigbag, Rip Rig and Panic, Maximum Joy, Glaxo Babies and Scream and Dance, who tended to call on the same revolving troupe of personnel. Where Pigbag were into Afro-funk and James Brown horn riffs, Rip Rig and Panic were named after a Roland Kirk album and flirted with free jazz and avant-garde sloganeering. Rip Rig and Panic also featured the young Neneh Cherry (and at one point her stepdad Don Cherry, the former Ornette Coleman Quartet trumpeter), who had also recorded with Mark Stewart and Ari Up of the Slits as the New Age Steppers on Adrian Sherwood's On-U Sound label. Many of the most important relationships which would later influence the direction of the Bristol hip-hop scene, especially the connection with Cherry, were thus established at this time.

The Pop Group

Listening to the products of Bristol's boho-punk contingent now is vaguely troubling; you want to like them but they don't make it easy for you. There are people in Bristol who will tell you in all good faith that the Pop Group were the greatest band they ever saw,

'Capitalism is the most barbaric of all religions ...' A Pop Group publicity still for their first album, 1979

but as Dave Higgitt, the editor of *Venue*, says, 'You really had to be there.' In the context of their era, however, the group were truly revolutionary, their music so extreme that it has managed to escape the punk–nostalgia boom of the present very easily; you might – at a push – pogo to the Pop Group, but you had to be able to think on your feet as you did so. There is at least as much attitude and ideas in their recordings – reflecting the CND and anti–fascist movements of the time, as well as elements of Situationist philosophy – as there is music, and though the bravado gestures don't easily translate to the nineties, only rarely can a group have said so much, so loudly, with so little musical knowledge to back it up, yet to such dramatic effect, as the Pop Group.

Their first single was 'We are All Prostitutes'

coupled with 'A Report on British Army Torture of Irish Prisoners' (Rough Trade, 1979), a conjunction you would love to have heard 'Fluff' Freeman announce on *Pick of the Pops*. Consisting of a funk-guitar riff, accompanied by mad saxophone and intensely irritating cello from free-jazz player Tristan Honsiger, Mark Stewart screams over the top: 'Capitalism is the most barbaric of all religions/department stores are our new cathedrals/our cars are martyrs to the cause/we are all prostitutes.' The B-side features distressing percussion and an Irish voice reading from Amnesty International's catalogue of torture by the British forces in Northern Ireland.

Their first album, *Y* (Radar, 1979), co-produced with dub reggae star Dennis Bovell (and recently re-released on CD), is pretty much more of the same, featuring a tribal-chic cover and the famous photo-journalism image of a Vietnam execution printed on the record's label. Playing it now conjures up an instant trip back in time to the DIY punk aesthetic of the late seventies, though it has to be said that much of the album sounds almost unlistenable today. Some of it is also very good, and it is true that the Pop Group were funky, after a fashion. Though they were part and parcel of the spirit of the age, they were also ahead of their time, using avant-garde elements of found sound through the inclusion of radio excerpts, pre-dating Brian Eno and David Byrne's influential album *My Life in the Bush of Ghosts*, and looking forward to the era of sampling and Tricky's rough collages of disparate bits and bobs.

The follow-up album, catchily titled *For How Much Longer Do We Tolerate Mass Murder* (Rough Trade, 1980), features a cover of two children kissing, surrounded by a montage of news cuttings about nuclear war, and it came complete with very impressive agitprop insert posters dealing with global conspiracies, a subject that was to become leader Mark Stewart's special subject, and a cinch if ever he made it on to *Mastermind*. The Pop Group linked up with their allies, the female punk group the Slits, in a single from 1980, with the Pop Group's contribution, 'Where There's a Will', being notable for lumpen reggae and funk riffs, including an attempt at a Chic-style 'Good Times' pattern, only slightly hampered by lack of musical ability. The single 'She is Beyond Good and Evil' was perhaps the Pop Group's finest moment and coming very close to the sound of their Manchester colleagues Joy Division, who weren't exactly a barrel of laughs either.

Boho Funk

Pigbag must still be collecting royalties from their one big number, 'Papa's Got a Brand New Pigbag', from 1981, which frequently crops up on television as an accompaniment to sports programmes, and has been remixed as a dance tune. Like the then-contemporary sound of New York's James Chance and the Contortions, it's James Brown sex-machine music refracted through an ironic sensibility, and joined haphazardly to Fela Kuti tribal funk. Rip Rig and Panic were the Pop Group's Gareth Sager again and Bruce Smith, pianist Mark Springer – who aspired to play atonally like Cecil Taylor – Sean Oliver on bass, and Neneh Cherry on vocals. Expressionistic, gestural funk in a cack-handed James Brown vein, with screaming punk-slogan vocals and sudden lurches into free-jazz piano, their debut album *God*, (with a cover photo of a baboon, natch) is hard to listen to now, though once again, people will swear to you that they were the best group they ever saw.

The Pop Group's Dan Katsis went on to form Glaxo Babies, whose 1980 single 'Shake (the Foundations)' is more than passable funk, with a Chic-type chorus and an instrumental B-side that could quite easily pass muster as a dance tune by the likes of Red Snapper

Pigbag: Wurzel funk in a boho style

today'. Katsis, together with the Pop Group's John Waddington, also formed Maximum Joy, who continued with more of the funk thang; their album of 1982, *Station M.X.J.Y.* was produced by Adrian Sherwood. Scream and Dance, whose single 'In Rhythm' coupled with 'Giacometti' from 1982 represents the later, softer, side of the Clifton–boho sound, mixed string bass with bongos and female voices in a way that looked forward to the beatnik–chic of Sade and Everything But The Girl.

Forced to summarize the Bristol sound of the bohemian punk and funk bands, you would have to say that their ideas exceeded their execution by a considerable distance, which was, of course, in keeping with the times. But what remains evident in their music is the strong undertow of black–music forms,

Rip Rig and Panic: Gareth Sager (left, foreground); Mark Springer (standing, looking normal); Sean Oliver and Neneh Cherry (*photo*: Panny Charrington)

of reggae, funk and jazz, and the aesthetic – only partly accounted for by punk – of a deliberate sonic roughness, a delight in the distressed patina of their sound, that does translate into the first examples of Bristol hip-hop.

Mark Stewart

Mark Stewart is an extraordinary figure who, more than anyone else on the scene, offers a link between the punk days of the late seventies, the sympathetic identification with reggae that followed, and the eventual arrival of the hip-hop sound systems that led to the Wild Bunch, Smith and Mighty, Massive Attack and Tricky. With a career poised somewhere on the mid-point between Nietszche on the one hand and Grandmaster Flash and the Furious Five on the other, Stewart has a lot to answer for. It was he who joined the German philosopher to the genre of the teenage love song in 'She is Beyond Good and Evil', and he who brought over to Britain the funkiest rhythm section in the world – the Sugarhill gang from the early New-York rap records – and then poisoned them with post-structuralist ideas, making them record on albums with titles like *As the Veneer of Democracy Starts to Fade.*

Stewart has been a cult item for so long that his reputation has begun to exude the *gravitas* of some venerable old figurehead for mutant musics of various kinds, a godfather to the avant-garde noise scene or the soldiers of the Bristol trip-hop tendency, and grandaddy to the newly resurgent apostles of dub, responsibility for any of which he denies. In fact, at thirty-five – he was born in 1960 – he's younger than some of his conceptual grandchildren, and though much of the music world has now caught up with what he was doing ten years ago, he's still in search of new, forbidden marriages between alien forms, like Eastern-European thrash metal and Norwegian techno, or American neo-noise bands and Balearic post-rave, that remain beyond the pale for most sensible listeners.

And in live performance Stewart remains a unique experience, a demonic figure to outdo Johnny Rotten, leading his troops into the heaviest collision of dub noise and funk beats imaginable. When, in May 1996, he returned to Bristol to play the Thekla with his group the Maffia, it was an auspicious occasion, with most of Bristol's musical aristocracy there to see him, though naturally they remained in the bar for the

Mark Stewart: he brought over the funkiest rhythm section in the world and then poisoned them with post-structuralist ideas

duration of the performance. It was also the loudest gig I have ever attended, the volume reaching quite distressing levels, and generating a ringing in the ears lasting for days to come. As a frontman Stewart was incredibly effective, even when wandering around the stage with a tea towel stuck to his head, his impossibly tall figure generating an atmosphere of considerable menace and excitement as the monstrous sound pinned you to the spot with a frightening, malevolent force.

Stewart's music, either with the Pop Group, or afterwards in his long, eccentric and commercially mostly unrewarding solo career, has often flirted with the unlistenable to the extent that it can actually be painful to hear his records. He also has the reputation of being completely mad. 'Whatever you do, don't mention helicopters', said Dave Higgitt when I mentioned that I was going to interview him; 'Or secret underground concentration camps in Wiltshire', said another *Venue* writer. They said it with affection too, but they said it all the same, for Stewart has been dogged with the reputation of a crazy man ever since his days as leader of the Pop Group. If you could do a word search on his press cuttings file, 'paranoid' would top the list of entries easily. A concern with data systems, disinformation and global conspiracies, and a screaming, hectoring vocal style, the voice sometimes distorted through a megaphone, have characterized his work, alongside a remarkable ability to latch on to forms of music just beginning to bubble up from the underground. After the fractured funk and punk aesthetic of the Pop Group, he formed the first version of the Maffia, a band made up of the heaviest reggae players on the British scene, collaborating with the On-U Sound producer Adrian Sherwood to create ridiculously bass-heavy, dubbed-up sound scapes, his inimitable vocal scream and obscure lyrical mannerisms ('expressionist' is a favourite critical description) working against the text of the otherwise palatable music.

Shortly afterwards he made contact with the rhythm section behind the early Sugarhill rap releases by Grandmaster Flash and the Furious Five, Keith LeBlanc, Doug Wimbish and Skip McDonald, making them his new Maffia. These musicians also went on to work as the Tackhead Sound System, recording on On-U Sound with Stewart's mate, the Barton Hill scaffolder and all-round general bad-boy Gary Clail, another ancestor of the Bristol sound. Stewart and Clail together made for an odd couple. It's said that Stewart, a middle-class chap who lived in carefully distressed bohemian squalor, was shocked on first encountering the working-class Clail's impeccably tidy flat, with its full complement of shiny consumer durables. The son of a publican from St Paul's, Clail had developed a reputation as a serious criminal and all-purpose nutter who would dare himself to perform gratuitous and possibly dangerous acts, like taking hold of the microphone at a St Paul's blues dance to toast, reggae style, declaring that he was the only white man with bottle in the house. Clail's career in music began, it is said, when Stewart bet him that he couldn't get a record released.

In 1987 Stewart produced what could be the first fully-realized document of what was to become the Bristol sound, when he took a version of Satie's 'Gymnopedie Number 1' by the producers Smith and Mighty, added his own alienating vocal, with lyrics and a melody line culled from Leonard Bernstein and Stephen Sondheim's 'Somewhere' from *West Side Story*, and called it 'Stranger Than Love', bunging Smith and Mighty five-hundred pounds and claiming the track as his own. It's a remarkable recording, the primitive drum-machine rhythms and clockwork-keyboard sounds set to exactly the kind of slow, slack pace that was the favoured tempo of the Wild Bunch's 'The Look of Love', Smith and Mighty's 'Walk On By' and 'Anyone', Massive Attack's 'Any Love' and the first recordings of Tricky. Only the mad, screaming voice made it unmistakably a Stewart track.

Later still, he shared a flat with Tricky and encouraged his first recordings. His punkish, bash-it-down-regardless, attitude to recording, and a willingness to break the normal boundaries of good taste, were also a notable influence on his protégé, whom he had known since the young delinquent was fifteen. In the mid-eighties the DJs, rappers and aspiring musicians of the Wild Bunch would hang out with him in the Dug Out and other Bristol clubs, and he blagged them an early sound-system appearance at the Language Lab club in London. Steve Haley, who now runs the Vision Factory studio where Smith and Mighty are based, remembers Stewart coming in one day to use a double-cassette machine. As he transferred the contents of one tape to another, he took care to ensure that the volume level was sufficiently high to send the LEDs completely into the red, achieving maximum distortion. When Haley asked what he was doing, Stewart replied that he was preparing the final master tape for his new album.

Sitting on the train to London on the way to interview Stewart, I listened to a tape of his new album on my Walkman. It was strong stuff, well within the usual parameters of the Stewart sound world, and I kept turning the volume down so that the leakage from my headphones wouldn't offend the other passengers, until the dial was almost at zero and I realized that it was myself I was protecting. At the Embassy Hotel in Notting Hill, where Stewart had been billeted by his record company, Mute, to do press for the release of the album, Stewart is disconcertingly normal, friendly and helpful and not at all paranoid, though he instructs a photographer from the *Melody Maker* to select only a few of the best prints to send to the paper: 'Don't let them have anything that can make me look paranoid, mate, 'cause if they can, they will. You know, nothing where I'm like looking madly at some spot on the ceiling.' The photographer assures him that he can be relied upon and Stewart starts to relax. He's just flown in from Ibiza (where he lives) that morning and his talk rebounds like a pinball from one conceptual bumper to another, occasionally nudged back up the table by the flipper of a new question.

MARK

The thing is with the Pop Group stuff is that I've vetoed it, up until now. Every year people from America, people from Japan, keep saying they want to re-release things and I vetoed it because to some extent it's like some poem I wrote to a girl in a youth club, a little love letter, you know, where the rhymes are rubbish and we were like sixteen. When I did my O–levels I'd just come back from a tour of Europe with Patti Smith about an hour before the exam, and I wrote this forty–page thing about Hamlet as the hero of the mind like I was on speed or something. It's not really relevant to me now and I'm so pedantic anyway that even this record I've just finished isn't really relevant because I'm always off on some new kind of hybrid. To me, it's only because we've reclaimed all the copyrights and we've been through all these intellectual copyright battles, and I've traced all the five members of the band, and it's been democratic and we've got total control of it, that I'll let it come out now. And then only because there's about twenty–thousand bootlegs in Japan and a couple of the band are on the dole. But I'm not really gonna push it. It's a period piece. I had to listen to a test pressing the other day and it was like, within a year or two I was already off on to something else. I'm not one of those people who sits around looking at old photos of myself and listening to old records, I've better things to do.

My basic attitude towards life hasn't really changed since I was about fourteen. The same kind of bolshiness, and the arrogance and not being able to be tied down, it hasn't changed. So maybe someone who's sixteen or seventeen, if they're going through all that teenage–angst stuff, they might be able to relate to it, but I can't. And people keep on referring to you as founder of this scene or godfather of that, or whatever, which immediately puts me off. I just do it because I want to do it, and then I'm off on to something else. I mean, so what?

There's a continuity in the work through the fact that it's me howling over the top of it, but I'm as influenced by other things as people are influenced by me. And so, for example, with this new album. I'm really excited by it because there's so much brilliant new music and I'm able to bring in technoid things that are as exciting for me as when we did all those dub or hip–hop crossover things we did in the past. So I'm listening to things like Fear Factory, Underground Resistance, all this brilliant techno or thrash metal and I just think 'Oh, I really like that drum sound on that German techno thing', and so that's the kind of music I'm trying to create. Not that I'm trying to copy anything, but I'm a magpie, I draw things from all over the place. I can only make music when I'm excited about it.

It's like when I was a soul boy back in Bristol. The

whole Bristol sound thing goes back to a thing called the Avon Soul Army, and the people who are growing up in Bristol now, it was like their big brothers used to dress up in Oxford bags and do crazy dancing to classic Ohio Players or Funkadelic stuff. And I grew up on the edges of a lower middle–class area but just down the road was St Paul's. So all the kids that went to football or youth clubs would be mixing together, and Bristol was small enough that things weren't as ghettoized as they would be in Manchester or Birmingham or London, and we'd all mix, and the only late–night club to go to would be a blues. I loved reggae and funk as much as I loved Iggy and the New York Dolls, so I never saw a difference in it. And now, drawing on things like Underground Resistance and some of the brilliant sounds coming out of the post–techno scene or the post–Balearic scene, it's as exciting for me as nicking stuff off an old King Tubby record.

The roots of the Pop Group were pre–punk. What was happening with the punk scene in England is the same as techno now, in isolation. I remember talking to Ian Curtis (of Joy Division), and there were people in Manchester, people in London, Wales, Scotland, who were coming up out of things like Cockney Rebel, who to me were brilliant. And John Cale did a couple of tours. It was coming out of finding these records like the dub stuff or weird kinds of metal–machine music, just finding things in isolation and buying them. And we had this idea, me and this mate of mine who was in a band called the Cortinas and is now a professor of semiotics, Jeremy Valentine – we were buying records in junk shops and just listening by ourselves. And then we'd go up to London shopping for fifties clothes and go to this place called Let It Rock, around the time all these bands were forming and McClaren was managing the Dolls. Somebody asked me to join this band which later became the Damned because I had an overcoat on or something, but in all these towns in Britain people were in isolation and then suddenly the Pistols came out. It was coming out of fashion, clubbing or something and it was more the audience than the music. You had to work to find stuff, you had to go through the racks, find a kindred spirit, and it was a real bond. It was still in advance of the *NME*. The kids were creating it, which is happening with a lot of the dance stuff now as well. People talk about the politics of it but the politics isn't in the lyrics, it's in the fact they're controlling the means of production, working their own vans, starting their own record labels, selling directly to their mates.

In like 1976 we'd go to the Arnolfini bar with our punk clothes on – it was the only place where you could go in the centre with punk clothes on without getting beaten up – and me and Simon Underwood, who was working at Rolls Royce, and Pete Summers, we were talking and I said we've got to get a band together. And we did, but we couldn't play. We thought we were as funky as the Ohio Players or Funkadelic but because we couldn't play all these older journalists like Richard Williams and Neil Spencer were coming up to us and saying we were avant–garde and sounded like Captain Beefheart. I couldn't stand Captain Beefheart, some jitter from school with his Grateful Dead records loved Captain Beefheart. They were saying we were avant–garde and all this but we thought we were in time!

I don't see politics as different to anything else. People ask me about politics and through the crap, English white–boy media I've been portrayed as this paranoid schizophrenic and my only saying to that lot is that a paranoid is someone who's in possession of all the facts. And I'm more interested in real history than I am in conspiracy theories, and I've put a lot of research into this stuff. My inquisitive nature towards politics is the same as my inquisitive nature towards finding an old reggae record. And for me there's no difference, and the only reason I'm termed a political singer is that the vast majority of other lyricists in the music game I think ignore ninety per cent of life. Not being rude, but for me to do that I'd have to wake up in the morning and put on a blindfold and a muzzle.

I see myself as writing a letter to somebody and being like a journalist reporting from the front line on how I see things. I'd be interested in all kinds of weird science and real history conspiracy theories or biotech or literary developments and whatever, even if I wasn't in a band. As to where my style of singing comes from, fuck knows. That's just me, I'd have been saying the same things in the pub, even if I wasn't in a band I'd be arguing in pubs, it's just my way of communicating my information. And the howling thing; to me the music has to be as important as the voice. It's like a little playlet or something.

Over the years I've made so many friends all over the world and they send me these classified documents, weird magazines about vapour wear, conspiracy 'zines, Vodka Cola deals, all these weird things which explode the history you were taught at school. All I'm saying is that I find this information interesting and that I'm going to make it available. I'm an 'informatician' as much as a musician. I've always been interested in information as much as anything and I thought music was the best way to communicate it. There's no such thing as politics – since the twenties the idea of the nation state has been obliterated. It's corporations – all the nation states do is administer the road building and the health services. It's economics, all politics is economics. I mean, I couldn't write a song about being sorted for Es and whizz. Not that it's my job to knock other individuals ...

What's interesting for me is that I have never really changed my position. I'm experimenting with new forms as much as I've ever experimented with them; but some of the music scene in England has moved round towards me, with things like Tricky taking off, with things like Nine Inch Nails being number one in America. For a kid of sixteen, the first club he would have gone to is an acid house club, so people's ears are more open to the kind of weird music I've been making for years, and, like one of my little cousins who's into jungle, they're getting back into dub through jungle. People's ears are a lot more open, even for things like what Björk is doing; Björk'll get Black Dog to do a mix, she'll work with a jungle kid; there's no underground or overground anymore. And with Trent being number one in America – before it would have been a little White Noise or Throbbing Gristle record, you know? It's good.

What's very good for the Bristol thing at the moment is that, coming from the hip–hop tradition around 1982 and the Dug Out the people are more into the beats, like Massive and Tricks and all that lot. The thing I like about it is they're not getting carried away with the stardom thing; like they'll work with Madonna one day and play in the back of a pub in St Paul's on a Saturday night still. And what I find really interesting is like DJ Die and Amos and Andy, the stuff just below Roni Size that they're doing in Steve Haley's studio, and it's like friends of my little brother's are coming out with this jungle stuff and they're

(OPPOSITE) 'All the nation states do is administer the road building.' Mark Stewart in 1996 (*photo:* Joe Dilworth)

talking about it in Japan. The Bristol thing is more organic, with respect back to the reggae sound system.

Years ago the Pop Group was the first indie–dance crossover. Buying a Prince Jammy or a Scientist dub thing was as important as buying Television or Patti Smith. I've always loved that stuff, even before rock music I've always loved brilliant funk, brilliant reggae, fucking hip–hop. I'm just as much a disco kid as I am an indie kid. There was this record shop in Bristol (still is) called Revolver, down on the Triangle, and we used to knock off school when we were about fourteen, fifteen, go for a smoke round a mate's house and every Friday we'd go to Revolver to listen to the new reggae pre–releases, right? We used to talk about this van from Zion that every Friday would bring the pre's. Revolver would only stock so many records but I was heavily into the dub stuff so as the two lads in the shop were playing through the pre's to see which ones to stock, we'd check the dubs to try and find which ones we wanted.

Three or four years later through links with Prince Far–I and Prince Hammer and the Slits, I got Adrian to give me a hand when the Pop Group were doing this massive CND demonstration at Trafalgar Square, which I was organizing as much as anyone. I wanted to do a song that the older socialists would know as much as the punky kids, so I decided to do a version of 'Jerusalem', and I got Adrian to mix it live in front of 55,000 people. And then it turns out that it was Adrian delivering on the van to Revolver, it was his first driving job and he was bringing the dubs down to Bristol when he was eighteen or nineteen.

And later, the first form of Mark Stewart and the Maffia was a disjointed reggae thing and the musicians we had were the heaviest Jamaican rhythm section living in England, and they recorded on On–U for Adrian. Then, through Grant and the Bristol hip–hop scene, when in 1981 to 1982 there was a very strong hip–hop tradition in Bristol which didn't even come to London, I made the connection with the Sugarhill gang. Nellee and Grant would be DJing at the Dug Out and we'd all be playing each other's parties, and whenever anyone went to New York to buy trainers or twelve–inches, they'd always tape the WBLS and Kiss FM radio shows from over there. Anyway, I got hold of this tape of Red Alert, this brilliant scratcher radio DJ, off WBLS. I think I got it from Grant, and there was this particular track on it that was this brilliant kind of industrial hip–hop drum machine with the sound effect of a rocket taking off over the top of it. I kept playing it to Adrian in the studio when we were trying to do this reggoid, duboid, sort of thing, trying to copy it, and by chance Adrian went to the MIDEM business fair to try and get some licensing deals for On–U and, by chance again, just across the precinct from him was Tom Silverman from the Tommy Boy label. Adrian's chatting to him in the course of the day, like you would at a car boot sale or something, and he says that this crazy mate of mine from Bristol is mad about some of your stuff. So Tommy gives Adrian Keith LeBlanc's phone number, we talk on the phone and we get Keith, Doug and Skip over to England. Keith had just done the Malcolm X thing, 'No Sell Out', and I think they were pleased to be able to experiment a bit, even though those four–four rhythms they did for 'White Lines' and stuff is an art in its own right; but they were quite pleased to get out of the studio, and we've just been hitting it off since then.

My methods of composition are the same as back in the Pop Group days, when I was doing things with double cassettes and stolen voices. I was editing and sampling on double–cassette machines before samplers were invented. Me and Adrian did one song where we had seventy-eight edits of bits of tape stuck on the studio wall, it was like *musique concrète*. Technology is there to be abused you know? I'd be doing it with spoons.

The 'Stranger Than Love' thing came about through Steve Haley, who in 1987 put on this event round the back of the Hippodrome called the Apres–Ski Party, which was the first time he persuaded Smith and Mighty to perform live. I was there with Tricky, who I'd known since he was at school, and Rob and Ray started playing their version of Satie's 'Gymnopedie Number 1', which I'd always loved and used to play. It was just another sense of synchronicity and I'd always checked Rob and Ray and respected the fact that they weren't pushy and they weren't trying to look at each other's trainers all the time. And I pushed Tricky on stage, which was the first time anybody got him to rap publicly, and then I started singing as well, and something just clicked. And that tune just meant so much to me, even though it's more Ray and Rob's tune than it is mine. I changed it around to a certain extent, but it just happened, and it's difficult for me to analyse how

things happened from a distance. But it was good. I think
Rob and Ray should get a lot more respect because they
were the first people to mess about with Dionne Warwick
things, like on 'Walk On By', and they were the founders
of that Bristol trip–hop scene as much as I was. Ray's like
Bim Sherman and some of my Rasta mates, they mumble
and you can't understand, but if you just sit down and
have a smoke with Ray and just listen to what he's
saying, he's the man, you know?

But going back, the creator of the Bristol scene is Miles
Johnson. This friend of mine Beezer is living in Japan and
I said it's really funny, someone's doing this book on the
Bristol scene, and he said well, he should speak to the
fucking king in exile. Just to give you a slight overview on
the whole thing, how everybody was growing up and
checking each other for the dress sense and confidence,
Miles was cool. I don't know how to explain this, but Miles
was cool, 'cos we all used to dress up, all these kit chaps,
Foster's lads, we all used to dress up in zoot suits, and the
scene kind of comes out of that. When you're a lad you
look up to these people and I was going down to these kind
of clubs and things when I was about fourteen, because I
was tall so I could always get in. Miles got banged up, I
think it was for football or something, and Nellee then was
a bit of a joke. So Miles came out of nick, he'd always had
a nice kind of fifties jacket but now he was really cool.

The Bristol thing is more in the way you stand, the way
you deal with your mates, but Miles was a really nice
bloke. All the girls liked him and all that kind of stuff but
he was just totally cool. And in the back bar of the Dug
Out there was all these little areas, I was over here with
all my mates from Knowle, I'd have my little table here
and Miles would just come in. But what happened was that
Nellee became Miles. Nellee was like this little kid from the
estates we'd see at Crass gigs or whatever, he wanted to be
mates with people and he was about this big and he was a
bit like Beezer, but Nellee clung on to Miles and some of the
cool rubbed off.

So the Wild Bunch were doing all this stuff and I was
coming up to London anyway through work, and I had all
these links with all these London arty–farty, white–boy funk,
hip–hop scenes, and there was a band called Funkapolitan,
from Maida Vale, and they were all fashion designers and
they were working for *ID* and all this stuff, right? And this
mate of mine James Le Bon had the first rap club in London

called the Language Lab and I was always going there, but it was all Maida Vale trustafarians. So I organized a battle between the Language Lab and the Wild Bunch and I got the Wild Bunch to come up and do their thing, like a sound–system battle in front of all these arty–farty London trendies. And then Nellee did another sound–system battle against Jazzy from the Soul to Soul sound system and then Nellee got in with Soul to Soul.

But just when you're younger and you have role models and you see how somebody stands, and whoever was the catalyst behind this thing, and I don't think I was, or only in the sense that they saw a fellow nutter going off and playing in Holland or America and they saw they didn't have to do some of the business stuff or whatever, Miles was the person who brought the hip–hop in and was a catalyst just by who he was and what he did. Everybody else looked up to him. Delge looked up to him, Grant was like a quiet boy from the suburbs to a certain extent, however they are portrayed, but I'm not trying to break anybody's image.

Even up to the Portishead thing, it all goes back to Neneh Cherry, you know? Because when we were first working with the Slits and when Neneh first came over she was like this Scandinavian punk. Miles used to have a Mohican as well, a little Mohican, but Neneh was just trying to get away from it all, chilling out in Bristol and that, and she and Cameron got their first deal and they sorted out all the style press, the *Face* and *ID* which really broke them, and which I'm missing out on coming from this indie angle. But Neneh was great.

The Wild Bunch

The Wild Bunch: the name still sounds gloriously heroic, conjuring up an image of rebel cowboys walking tall and talking tough in a funky, multi–ethnic, version of a Marlboro ad. Someone in the posse must have seen the Peckinpah film they named themselves after, or maybe they all did, sitting together in a row at the local Odeon one evening. Robert Del Naja remembers that when he joined he had to persuade the others to stop calling themselves the Wild Bunch Posse,

because, he argued, that was like saying the Wild
Bunch Bunch. The excellent photographs that were
taken at the time, by Beezer, Julian Monaghan and Rob
Scott, who memorialized the whole period very
effectively, show the group posing behind the decks at
the Dug Out. Nellee Hooper looks impossibly young
and baby-faced, Grant looks pretty much as he does
now; Del Naja stares out of the frame like the
precocious youth he was, trying to look as hard as his
namesake Robert De Niro, and Miles Johnson – well, he
looks like a star. 'I used to fancy him when he was
younger', remembers Sapphire, 'and that's why I used
to follow the Wild Bunch around. But I frightened him
once, when I got this pretty girl at the Dug Out to chat
him up, with an eye to coming back to my place for a
threesome. He came back but when he found out what
was involved he didn't want to know.'

The Wild Bunch formed around the scene that had
developed at the Dug Out in 1982 or so and comprised
Miles Johnson, Nellee Hooper, Grant Marshall, Robert
Del Naja (who joined later) and Claude Williams, and
later still, Andrew Vowles (Mushroom). They started to
DJ at the Dug Out, where Marshall was already
established, every Wednesday, and became Bristol's
first New York-style sound- system crew. Their
performances at illegal parties, such as on the downs,
where the police arrived to close them down, in
abandoned warehouses like the Red House in St Paul's,
at private parties, proper gigs like the Granary, or at St
Paul's carnival – where they played till dawn – soon
made them a legendary fixture of the Bristol scene,
attracting a loyal following that mixed black hip-hop
heads from St Paul's with Clifton trendies.

Hooper and Johnson manned the decks, specializing
in grandiose scratching of early hip-hop records such
as those on the Def Jam label, with Marshall also DJing

(Opposite) Grant Marshall and politically-incorrect Wild Bunch poster, 1986
(*photo*: Rob Scott)

and acting as MC, and Del Naja and Williams rapping. Del Naja was also a noted local graffiti artist, with several very public and illegally-decorated sites to his name, some dedicated to the Wild Bunch, and the group thus represented not only a form of music but an offshoot of the whole, integrated street culture of the new hip-hop movement, appropriating whatever they could learn about their New York predecessors into a set of attitudes and practices that were then transplanted to their home city.

They were also very disorganized and argued between themselves constantly. When, in 1985, shortly after the Arnolfini jam, I made a short video about them at the St Paul's flat shared by Johnson and Marshall, it was evident that there was a constant conflict. Del Naja was full of ideas but didn't have the necessary seniority to communicate them successfully to the others, and there was a continual air of tension. By this time they were also successfully on the blag, Del Naja appearing in a documentary about graffiti art being made by the director Dick Jewell for Channel Four, and getting his graffiti into a book by author Henry Chalfont, along with Goldie from Wolverhampton.

What happened between then, and the foundation of Massive Attack in 1988, is hard to relate without considering the different versions of the story told by the participants themselves, as they diverge on a number of points. I've therefore decided to let them tell their own story in their own words, the account of Miles Johnson, followed in the next chapter by that of Robert Del Naja. The essential facts are that in 1987 the Wild Bunch blagged a trip to Japan through contacts made via Neneh Cherry and *The Face* magazine. Del Naja was unhappy there and returned home, ending up being thrown out of the group. Johnson and Hooper then signed a deal as the Wild Bunch with Island records, with themselves as the only signatories, and recorded a couple of singles, including 'The Look of Love' and 'Friends and Countrymen', which were released by Island in America and on import in Britain. Johnson and Hooper, who were by now living in London, then fell out and Hooper went on to form Soul to Soul with Jazzie B, while Johnson went back to Japan and then to New York. Del Naja, Marshall and Vowles formed Massive Attack, conceived of as a Soul to Soul-type project and first mooted as an actual offshoot, to be produced by Hooper. Signed to a management deal by Cameron McVey, Massive then signed a recording contract with Virgin which eventually resulted in the *Blue Lines* album.

Miles

Miles Johnson now lives in New York with his Japanese wife and two small children, running a company exporting street-fashion clothes to Japan. He has continued to make music on a part-time basis and put out a few singles on his own label, but he hasn't spoken to Nellee Hooper, Robert Del Naja or Grant Marshall for eight years.

MILES

I went to Cotham Grammar, and that's when I met Willie [Claude Williams, the Wild Bunch rapper who was relegated to the role of a driver when Massive signed to Virgin], but he didn't come into the Wild Bunch until later. G, Nellee and me did a few things in the late seventies but mainly it was early eighties. Then I got stuck away in jail, in London, while Nellee was in Maximum Joy, and when I got out in 1982 we got together again and started doing parties in Clifton and stuff. In the late seventies, pre–hip–hop, we were playing basically reggae, soul, jazz fusion and punk, new wave. I'd never have called myself a punk but I liked Wire, PIL, and I know a little bit about the music – I don't discriminate except where it comes to country music. But punk was hip and there were things I liked about it, the creative stuff. In jail I listened to John Peel all the time and he said, 'This is what's happening in New York', and played 'Planet Rock'.

When I got out we started DJing at the Prince's Court

club, pre–Dug Out, and there was some input of hip–hop but as to the visual side we didn't have anything to go on, no videos or anything. When we did get to see a video, or maybe the film of *Wild Style*, it switched on every part of the information, the sneakers, the trousers, the graffiti, whatever.

Although hip–hop was American and we were British there was never that sense of not understanding it. We were West Indians dealing with reggae and they were dealing with soul, everyone had the same struggles, the same search for enjoyment. It was wild, cutting like that. What I liked about punk, although it sounded a bit fake, was the same as I liked about hip-hop – you didn't have a regular rhythm and you could be creative with it.

In the punk days we got this band together, me, Nellee, Paul Johnson and a couple of guys from Barton Hill, playing punk or new wave, and that was the first thing I ever did as a group, playing percussion. When I came out of jail Nellee came and started checking me – he was the only one who wrote me when I was inside – and we hooked up. We started doing things naturally and started buying records together. We were doing just parties in people's homes and getting our own equipment. When we started to work as a crew there'd be parties on the downs in the summer and St Paul's carnival where we used to set up, borrowing speakers, right on the front line. As to cutting up and stuff, I mean we didn't even know until *Wild Style*, and then it was, like, we got to get those turntables. We weren't the first in England, though we were pretty early. We did a little dub–plate recording and we used to play it and people really used to love it; it was just like a master plate, and we had to play it over and over again. It was original music recorded in a studio, with bass and drums, we may even have done it in London.

St Paul's carnival was the ultimate. We used to play till real early in the morning and we'd have the biggest set, the loudest system. We ventured up to London and played at Notting Hill carnival and we did a warehouse party with Nutriment and took a few coaches up there, stepped out in North London, but not like we rocked it in St Paul's. We were one of the best crews around, like Mastermind in London and we had a lot of music from the past, from back in the days, like funk and stuff. We also did the

(OPPOSITE) Miles Johnson at the Dug Out, mid-eighties (*photo*: John Hicks)

Language Lab with another crew, which was Mark Stewart's scene. We'd mix reggae with hip–hop but it would depend what crowd it was, it's not like we'd just stick to any format. The London crowd liked the hip–hop and the classic soul. The Bristol taste was different, you could drop some reggae in there. But the demographics of our crowd changed until we were playing just to Clifton types and students.

The warehouse parties in Bristol were amazing; the Red House was the first warehouse jam and that was massive. In 1986 Neneh Cherry called Grant's girlfriend – I was practising at the turntables at the time – and she said 'Neneh Cherry wants you to go to Japan.' I'd never been anywhere, never even had a passport. We went over there, played a couple of fashion shows, a couple of gigs, and then when I got back home I said we should go back. There were hard times and struggles but in the end we had fun. Neneh Cherry was with the guys from the *Face* and she got us involved with the top fashion designers, because the Buffalo–type image was strong at the time. What they were really after was good–looking black guys, or at least that's what it seemed to me. I knew Neneh from Bruce Smith, who I had known from my school. He was an American and he came to our school and they started picking on him, and basically, I stopped him getting a big hiding, and he always liked me after that.

When we came back from Japan it all started happening. At one time we were playing three clubs a week and because I used to work in London at Kensington Market during the week I used to have to travel back and forth. We'd do the Dug Out and the Tropic in Bristol and I'd have to go back to London to work in the morning. I also did a little bit of modelling for the cash, because it was good money.

3D? I don't like talking about that guy. I should have known about him. I liked him up to a certain time but after he left us and came back from Japan I thought 'Why'd he do it?' We fell out and I didn't speak to him when he was still in the crew. Everybody else kept on at me to speak to him and I did but I shouldn't have; he's a big part of what happened. As far as I was concerned me and Nellee and G were the Wild Bunch, Willie and 3D were just there for MCing. They were good and 3D's a talented writer, at that time I was astounded at some of the stuff he was writing, before he started taking mushrooms and stuff ...

Then me and Nellee moved to London and that was the big thing, but Grant and the others they didn't want to do it, preferring to stay big fish in small waters. You could say they were right and we were wrong, but we got the deal with Island and we wanted them to be part of the group. We stuck our necks out to go to London; we got an apartment and got a deal, the first British rap group to be signed to a major, but they wanted to stay where they were. We said, 'Why don't you come, do some music, get some ideas down?' There was always some kind of beef because me and Nellee were coming out of London ... I still don't really understand what happened for us to break up. Me personally, I think Delge had a lot to do with the split of the group. We were growing out of the mindset of being together but I was into getting something out of this break. Grant wasn't willing to sacrifice anything, and they weren't willing to see the possibilities. It was me and Nellee who went to Japan first; we didn't know where we were going to stay but we weren't bothered about that. I can't say I blame them but, you know, you only live once, you've got to take the opportunities.

Then I went back to Japan on my own, met a girl and I needed some time out of that scene as there were a few things that pissed me off about the Island deal. When I left, there was money in my bank account and when I came back it had gone. That was the falling out of me and Nellee; the guy was the biggest liar to the fullest extent. We were the most honest people in the whole crew but G took the view to believe Nellee and not me, and so me and G fell out. Basically it was about Massive Attack. I was in my sister's house and Nellee phoned and said he wanted to go into production, producing Massive Attack as a Soul to Soul offshoot, but I wanted my own identity, not Soul to Soul junior. I was upfront, Nellee got mad at me and I ain't spoke to him since for eight years. I'm happy for the geezer. It's good to see him where he is. I'm a bit sad Massive didn't do a bit better, though. I thought their record was a bit lightweight. I really believe it; it wasn't what I had imagined it would be. I thought it would be, like heavier, heavy bass–line music. 3D don't know anything about music, not like G knows his reggae; he's got no rhythm and I guess his influence was in there. The second album I haven't even heard.

I still stay in contact with Mushroom but he's really guarded about me hearing the stuff. Obviously, yeah, he was influenced by me. He was a cute guy and he had a passion for hip–hop, that's what we liked. I feel he's going to be a real successful guy, into the technical sounds and stuff like that. When it comes to sounds he's the man.

Tricky? he came to see me three years ago and we had a disagreement because he invited me over for a jam and then he didn't give me the money. I didn't even know he was large; I didn't want to know. I've seen him on a few magazines over here, the things that college people read like *The Village Voice*. I'm happy for him. He'll tell you – he can't be anything but honest – I used to teach him stuff through an old relative. I had an old girlfriend I was staying with and he was a cousin of hers.

G hasn't seen me for as long as Nellee has. I like G, he's a nice guy and he's got a heart of gold. He's an easygoing guy who doesn't want to do much to make a living. Is there a group called Portishead? Mushroom told me something about them and I saw their name somewhere and I couldn't make sense of it because I knew the place. English rap didn't take off; as for people in Bristol being special I don't know. It's kind of weird, why is it that all these groups have taken off? Smith and Mighty blew up first, Goldie, I know him, that's a real surprise. When I listen to jungle I just think man, get out of here. I like the beats played at the right speed. But the British music scene is the best in the world, the diversity, the charts ... I'm still doing music, that's my life. I've got about fifty DATs of stuff I've done on my computer; I should put them out. I did a few independent things and just finished a project with some guys in Harlem called Harlem High. I do music whenever I can. I play people my stuff but I haven't really tried shopping my music. I've done some house stuff for about three years and some hip–hop with rappers.

The business is me and my wife, not just me. I do a lot of running around, now we've got two kids.There's so much competition in the market, it's cool though, it pays the rent ... I said this year might be my year. Hopefully, I'll get over soon.

MASSIVE ATTACK

One night in May 1996, when I'm trying to finish this book, working on this very chapter, I go out to the pizza restaurant across the road and run into Grant and Mushroom right outside my front door, which is in the street next to the studio where Massive Attack are working on their new album. They're sitting in their cars, which are parked side by side, and they're talking to each other though the open windows. 'Where's Delge?', I say. 'Has he gone solo?' 'I tell you mate', says G, 'he soon will be.' 'He's dyed his hair', says Mushroom. 'Blue'. We chat for a bit, talking about the Mark Stewart gig at the Thekla a few days earlier. They're very amused at finding out where I live. 'Now we know where to come to burgle you', Grant says. I go to collect my pizza and they're still there when I return so we chat a bit more before they drive off.

I go back inside and imagine the scene outside the studio earlier as the three friends take their leave of each other, G and Mushroom getting into their cars while Delge waits for his cab or goes to the pub next door. 'See you tomorrow, mate,' they call, and then the two of them drive round the corner and park at a pre-arranged spot for a post-mortem on the day's activities. Do they, you wonder, do this every night? It could be like a trip-hop version of *Double Indemnity*, the former lovers caught in a cycle of deceit and intrigue, or a Tom and Jerry cartoon, each stalking the other with a murder weapon behind their backs; just as one is about to spring a surprise blow and bury the knife in the shoulder blades, the other (who is also carrying a hammer or a knife) comes along and they pretend to be mates again, talk about the weather and wait for the next murderous opportunity. Of course, this is all a fantasy projection, but they do argue a lot ...

Three Wise Men

There's a satisfying visual rhyme in the appearances of Massive Attack. Grant Marshall (Daddy G, or G for short) is very tall and very dark; Robert Del Naja (3D, D, Delge) is small, white and blonde. And in the middle, like the product of some strange union between the other two, is the medium-tall, light- brown Andrew Vowles (Mushroom). Their ages provide a different sort of rhyme. Marshall, as befits the daddy, is the oldest at thirty-five; Del Naja is thirty-one, Vowles the baby of the group at twenty-eight. Their temperaments are also in contrast to each other; Marshall is amiable and easygoing, though to outsiders like me he can be a little cool and remote; Del Naja is warm and friendly and very very talkative, Vowles quiet and self-contained. Their backgrounds are equally varied: Marshall's parents are Barbadian, Del Naja's father is Neapolitan, his mother English; Vowles has Spanish and Caribbean ancestry. Neither are from the rough end of town, St Paul's or the estates, unlike the other Wild Bunch members, Smith and Mighty or Tricky.

Their respective social worlds are also very different, and apart from the business of being in a group together they don't spend that much time in one another's company. Marshall is a working DJ and he plays regularly in Bristol and elsewhere, often in the company of Nick Warren (now half of the recording unit Way Out West and the DJ for the group's tours). Del Naja hangs out with his own mates and is a bit of

(OPPOSITE) And then there were three: Delge, Mushroom, Daddy G
(*photo*: Jeurgen Teller)

a lad, into beer and football; and Vowles doesn't hang out much at all, neither drinking, smoking nor drinking tea or coffee, though he DJs sometimes too.

In terms of a division of labour within the group, Vowles is the music-boffin, who does the main pre-production, assembling tracks in his home studio. Del Naja writes most of the lyrics and takes care of the visuals, collaborating on the packaging of their music and the design of the stage shows. Marshall, who has a huge collection of soul and reggae records, selects suitable candidates for sampling. Since the departure of their guest singers and rappers, he is also being called upon to perform more than in the past, though in the original Wild Bunch he was an MC as much as a DJ. On a television appearance in *The White Room* in early 1996, Marshall – who often seemed to be the most redundant member of the group – looked suddenly to have found his role, standing at the front with Del Naja, looking cool and speaking the rhymes that Tricky rapped on 'Karmacoma' with an impressive mixture of menace and charisma.

With their second album *Protection*, released at the end of 1994, Massive Attack re-established themselves after a period when it looked possible that they would break up. It successfully consolidated the critical acclaim of *Blue Lines*, sold much better than its predecessor and won them a Brit Award in 1996 for best dance act, when Del Naja's brief acceptance speech emphasized that none of them knew how to dance. At last, after a further attempt to tour as a sound system to promote *Protection*, they have bitten the bullet and gone out as a proper band with additional musicians, playing in Europe, America and Australia in 1995, and doing the rounds of the big European summer festivals in 1996.

A series of small triumphs has also given them a kind of *gravitas*, with the intelligent, dance-music-for-listeners genre they helped to pioneer, influencing a whole strain of hip acts who now name check them as precursors. They've even become revered figures with an impressive air of seniority, although their output has hardly been prolific. The success of Portishead and Tricky has inevitably been accompanied by further name checks for Massive, and the notion of the Bristol sound is usually traced back to them. They've recorded with Madonna on a version of 'I Want You' for the Motown Marvin Gaye tribute album, which also appeared on her greatest hits album; Tina Turner has covered 'Unfinished Sympathy', and following Tracey Thorn's collaboration with Massive on *Protection*, Everything But the Girl are more popular than ever before. They also manage to maintain a high profile in the style press without necessarily doing very much to justify it, and further projects that are in discussion, like a planned short film to be written by Will Self, ensure that they will continue to appear as a quality act. Even if it is never realized, the idea indicates discernment, like their videos directed by Baillie Walsh, which have established a cool, black-and-white aesthetic of superior, restrained values that stands out clearly amongst the dross of run-of-the-mill promos.

With a new management team behind them they are being marketed more carefully than before and their relationship with Virgin – their parent record company – is on a sure footing (though it's rumoured that they are still heavily in debt to the company), and a huge sum has been approved for their next album, which is planned to include a CD-ROM version. They are also to get their own label to act as a production base for new acts that they choose, and re-releases of works by their heroes, such as a projected series of *Legends of the Sound System* reggae compilations.

Massive Style

From their first appearance, when Massive Attack was briefly shortened to Massive by their record company because of the Gulf War, the group have always looked the part: styled by Judy Blame, photographed by Jean Baptiste Mondino, and linked to the Buffalo-Stance look associated with Neneh Cherry and popularized by *The Face*. 'Buffalo was the name of Ray Petri's gang', says Sheryl Garratt, who wrote for and then edited *The Face* over the period from 1987 to 1995. 'It was a group of models, stylists, musicians and photographers who went by that name and included Jamie Morgan, Cameron McVey – who began as a photographer with *The Face* – and Neneh. It was all about looking good and doing creative things and Massive were on the fringes of that world. But the main thing about all that Bristol music and what happened at *The Face* is that someone in Bristol released a record in January or February for three years running and you just knew that come the end of the year they would be at number one in our annual list. *The Face* is a magazine that runs on people's enthusiasms and we liked the music, right back to the Wild Bunch and 'The Look of Love'. Plus Lindsay Baker, who was an editorial assistant on the magazine, was going out with Grant so we got to hear all the stuff.

'A lot of people would play with reggae things at the time but Massive were more successful than most because they'd thought about image as well and hooked up with people like Mondino early on, plus they had a bit of an art background themselves. In the end most British groups like that didn't think much about how they looked and Massive – and I don't mean this in a mean way – they're not any great shakes to look at, but they'd designed an image for themselves. And compared to everything else that was going on, their records were really fresh-sounding, maybe because Bristol was a bit more insular. They just sounded really fresh and original, as if these people had had a vision and had followed it, without listening to everything else that was in the top ten or had been played in clubs up and down the country. You felt that here were a group of people who were evolving without thinking what fashion thought of it.'

Neneh Cherry

The association with Neneh Cherry was very influential. Her debut album *Raw Like Sushi* sold over two million copies worldwide and was the first hip-hop record by a female artist to really make an impact commercially, giving her production company

The Cherry Connection

Cherry Bear (founded with her partner Cameron McVey) considerable power. Cherry already had a Bristol connection through her work with Rip Rig and Panic, and together with their drummer, Bruce Smith, she had a daughter, Naima. Through connections established via *The Face*, as well as the earlier links with Bristol, Robert Del Naja was asked to work on lyrics for *Raw Like Sushi*, to which he contributed parts of 'Manchild', and Mushroom did some mixing on the record, later going on tour with Cherry as a DJ. With original Wild Bunch members Nellee Hooper involved with Soul to Soul, and Miles Johnson out of the country, the fledgling Massive Attack were signed up to a management deal by Cameron McVey, who funded the recording of *Blue Lines* and then got them a recording deal with Virgin.

Massive Reconstruction

Later, after the success of the *Blue Lines* album in 1991, and an abortive American tour as a sound system (both covered in the interview with Del Naja below), Massive Attack's world fell apart. Singer Shara Nelson resigned in favour of a solo career, Cameron McVey left them to go off to Spain with Neneh Cherry, and Tricky left to concentrate on his own album. Suddenly, there didn't seem much of Massive Attack left, and for a while it looked like they had been dropped by their record company in the wake of Virgin's takeover by EMI. Worse still, they fell out with each other. When Nelson left they placed an anonymous ad in *Melody Maker* to recruit a replacement. 'We gave a brief of Tracey Chapman and Aretha Franklin', says Del Naja, 'but all we got was tapes from these white country-and-western geezers.' 'It was terrible', says Marshall; 'There's probably a million brilliant voices out there and we got Billy Ray Cyrus soundalikes.'

Even while she was in the group, Nelson had

created problems, as she increasingly became identified as the principal presence. When they went on television to promote the singles from *Blue Lines* it was difficult for the three main men to know what to do with themselves. In one memorable appearance on the Jonathan Ross show they settled for skulking at the back pretending to play keyboards while a hired band played an approximation of the studio track with Nelson as the front person. 'Putting a sound system on television looks crazy', says Del Naja. 'You're meant to perform and we don't.'

The paradox of Massive is that although they come from a tradition of sound systems, the music they make is for listeners rather than dancers. They create their music on computer, piecing together patterns and samples from a floppy disc 'riff bank', and layering them to form sophisticated soundtracks which are then farmed out to carefully selected outworkers for further embellishment. The irony is that their digital methods have created a delicate kind of designer/maker music that seems more handcrafted than that of most pop artists. They are heavily reliant on others in translating their ideas to finished pieces of music, however, as when they get the engineer to see what they want out of a particular synth sound by getting him to play it and then saying, 'like, a bit more phwaah, please'.

Protection

They share the songwriting credits on their records, together with their collaborators, but the exact detail of who does what remains rather imprecise. On the title track of *Protection*, Vowles began, he says, 'with a drum track and a sample of a James Brown lick on a 808 bass drum. Then there was this Fender Rhodes riff I'd had lying around for ages that I got out of the old riff catalogue. It was all a bit jaggedy so I put some strings on it to smooth the whole thing out and added a spacy 303 bass line, which is one of those old acid bass lines they use in house records. I then thought it would need to build towards the end so I wrote a piano pattern to sort of go against everything else.' A tape of the song was dispatched by post to Tracey Thorn, whom Marshall and Del Naja had admired since her first solo album years ago, and who felt flattered at being asked to collaborate. 'We faxed her about fifteen pages of lyrics', Del Naja says, 'but she politely said she'd prefer to use her own.' Thorn wrote the lyric, recorded her demo vocal and sent the tape back; when she came into the studio to sing the final version it was completed in ten minutes. 'It was a real challenge for her to work with these loops and patterns', Vowles says, without irony, 'because normally she writes with like' – his voice rises to a mild note of incredulity – 'an acoustic guitar.' Vowles says he's keen to study music formally and would like to go to college but the others are sceptical, claiming it would give him an unfair advantage.

NELLEE HOOPER

The choice of Hooper to produce the album was an obvious one, though it didn't prove entirely helpful. A former member of the Wild Bunch, Hooper had become the most sought-after producer in the country, first working with Soul to Soul and then producing Sinead O'Connor's version of Prince's 'Nothing Compares to U', which topped the charts in America. After this he produced Björk's *Debut* album, one of the most startling records of the nineties, and as a consequence was recruited to work on Madonna's *Bedtime Stories*. By the time he got around to *Protection*, Hooper was perhaps the hippest record producer in the world. 'He knew he could have a lot of fun with it', says Del Naja, 'working with his friends, which worked against us because we wasted a lot of time. When he was working on Madonna's album it was nine to five every day; with us, we'd get to the studio about two in the afternoon, chat for two hours, do two hours work then get a takeaway in and go out for the night. He said he felt like Daniel Day-Lewis in *My Left Foot*; he couldn't do anything. He'd sit in the producer's position, reclining in a chair with a hangover. At certain points we said, "Look, we'll go back to Bristol, you do your thing"'. 'It never happened', says Marshall. 'Yes it did', says Del Naja, and they begin to argue again. In July 1994 Hooper invited Massive over to Dave Stewart's studio in California, where he was working on Madonna's *Bedtime Stories* album, to meet his new employer, and also to see the World Cup final. This led to some embarrassment because Massive, despite staying at a house in the studio, were, in Del Naja's words, 'so out of it' that they failed to get up each day in time to meet Madonna, who had departed by the time they arose. They were pressed by Hooper to phone her afterwards and apologize, and from this contact came the opportunity of working with her on the version of Marvin Gaye's 'I Want You'.

CRITICAL MASS

When Massive did eventually regroup for the long-awaited second album, they didn't have a lot of material to work with. The result is an ambiguous set that promises much but ultimately, perhaps, fails to meet the extremely high standards of their debut. On the one hand, it was another Massive Attack album, which everyone wanted, and there was an enormous amount of goodwill hanging over from the brilliance of *Blue Lines*; on the other, there wasn't an awful lot there. The soundtrack elements which were made much of by the critics didn't really amount to very much; two instrumentals that sounded rather unfinished, as if still waiting for the vocals to be added, and the rich orchestral arrangements on the vocal

The *Protection* Sound System Tour at Bristol's Ashton Court Mansion, 1995:
Claude and Mushroom. (OPPOSITE) Live at the Phoenix Festival, summer 1996
(*photo*: Mick Hutson)

features for Nicolette, their new guest singer, were
perhaps too similar to Talvin Singh's string arrangements for Björk's *Debut*.

The most appealing songs, the only real songs on
the album perhaps, were the two numbers with lyrics
and vocals by Tracey Thorn, 'Better Days' and the
beautiful 'Protection' itself, which had a satisfying

tension between the emotional intensity of the lyrics, the technical skill of their delivery, and the cool, disembodied, machine-music of the backing tracks. Tricky's contribution, the rap 'Karmacoma', was also effective, with the industrial beats of the galloping rhythm standing out against the rather clean and clinical sound of the rest of the album.

It's still a good-ish album, but unlike *Blue Lines* the songs didn't really scratch the soul of the listener, although they have enjoyed a healthy commercial afterlife as mood music, where the overall mood is a rather detached one, functioning well as superior background noise to be played in the kitchen or the car. The smooth finish of the sound is, however, beautifully done and the production somehow creates a sensation of lushness while still managing to retain a minimal feel through its sparing use of resources. Compared to everything else around though, *Protection* was still a very superior product, and it suggested numerous new directions for the band, from film scores to sophisticated, after-dinner-mint soul.

The critical reception for *Protection* was generally very favourable. In fact you could almost argue that the record had been designed to achieve just that effect; teasing the listener with the promise of a deepening meaning and then, after the review was written or the album bought and paid for, frustratingly refusing to go the whole way. It was difficult not to think that Massive had spent more time doing press for the album than they had in actually making it. The press-cuttings book is almost two inches thick, and they did everything, from the qualities to the style press to the listings mags around the country. A whole series of journalists and photographers was brought down to Bristol for a rendezvous with the group at the Swallow Royal hotel, where, amid the velvet-flock wallpaper and chintzy sofas of the lounge, the interview or the photo shoot was consummated.

ORIGINAL VERSION

Despite the huge regard in which Massive Attack are held by their fans, their contemporaries and the critics, there remains an air of doubt about what exactly it is that they have done to achieve their success. About how, to put it bluntly, three non-musicians have managed to create such strong, sustaining music. Rumours exist about the exact roles of their collaborators and the extent to which it is their contributions, rather than those of the remaining three members of the group, that have been responsible for the final product, although this argument begs the question of how pop music these days is produced. In a world of digital samplers and computer programs for composing, the whole notion of the creative process has changed and Massive Attack's main talent may well, in the final analysis, be their taste, which seems fair enough as long as they continue to acknowledge their collaborators. Disagreements, though, do occur, and Paul Johnson insists that he composed and played the bass line on the title track of *Blue Lines*, but only received a flat fee for his efforts.

Two of the tracks on *Protection* - 'Karmacoma' and 'Eurochild' - were produced with the help of the Insects, a Bristol-based unit formed by Bob Locke and Tim Norfolk to do mainly soundtrack work, and evolving out of an earlier Bristol band, the Startled Insects, who in the mid-eighties performed in weird masks and costumes at multi-media events, and made two albums for Island Records. When Massive began recording for *Protection*, they, together with Tricky came to the Insects' studio in Redland to do some work, and later returned to record what was to become 'Karmacoma'. 'The very first loop was from an Indian-soundtrack album that Tricky had brought in', says Locke, 'and we took it from there. Probably that same evening Tricky and 3D laid down about sixteen tracks of rapping until the overall track was about ten minutes long. Then it was just left lying around for a couple of months, so me and Tim went back to it and picked out the best bits of the raps, arranged it and put the whole track together on our own. They didn't ask us, we just did it, and then we posted it to them. They said they liked it and we just carried on and did "Eurochild."'

The Insects now share space in the same studio as Massive in Christchurch, Clifton, a former BBC studio now taken over and let out into units by the owner of the Coach House. 'What happens is that we'll work on things and generate ideas with them', says Norfolk. 'It's an extremely informal relationship and it's good fun because we really like their stuff. We don't try and think "this is Massive Attack, this is the Bristol sound", we just do what we want and if they like it, great.' 'What they end up with, who knows', says Locke. 'We don't know what our contribution will be until the album comes out, really.'

Delge

Robert Del Naja opens the door to his flat to let you in, keeping up a constant stream of talk as he shows you through to the living room, past the wall which is full of robot toys and books in the hall, past the television and play station in the lounge, showing you the crack in the ceiling, asking if you want a cup of tea. He can't stop moving. He asks if you want tea again and puts the kettle on, asks you if soya milk is ok, asks if you've seen the cat, asks if you want tea again. He takes you outside to show you his painting studio, then worries in case the cat has got in and will get trapped. Spray-painted canvases litter the floor. He's just sold one to James Lavelle, he says, though he charges him full whack because he's got loads of money. He checks for the cat again, asks if you want tea then forgets about it again as you sit down at the kitchen table to choose pictures for this book from his files. You go through each page, making a preliminary selection, he vetoing anything that he thinks is too posey or unflattering, putting markers between the pages of the ones that make it through the selection process.

He asks about tea again, then forgets once more and, just as you're about to go out together to the shop to photocopy the pictures, he has second thoughts. There's not going to be that many pictures, is there, he says, and the other bands will be represented too, so maybe it's best not to choose so many, better to select only those that really might make it into the final edit. So, painstakingly, you go through the files again, he ruling out this one and that as too posey again, too dark, too red, too young- looking, until there's only a quarter of the original quantity left.

Then we leave for the shop in my car, talking about football. We take several wrong turnings, he forgetting to say where we're going, and once settled on a route we over-shoot the destination because he's distracted and forgets. After we've left the pictures to be copied he blags a lift to an army-surplus shop downtown, where he's seen a neat one-piece combat suit that might just do for his forthcoming appearance at the Brit Awards. He always wears combat-type clothes and always has done, going back to the military-chic days of the Clash. In the shop, he looks at the suit doubtfully, wonders whether he should buy it, and then takes the plunge, forking out the fifteen quid or so, and I take him back to the centre, where he's got to go to John Lewis to buy a vacuum cleaner.

Delge worries, and he takes the responsibilities of the other band members on his shoulders and worries for them too. If you try to get him on the phone around noon, the time he's likely to be up, it's constantly engaged, sometimes for hours, as he vanquishes the guilt of his hangover and the non-productive time he spent yesterday by manically making calls to sort out his business affairs. There'll be his Fantasy Football team to worry about, last night's results to catch up on, videos of Italian football games to watch, appointments to make, people to see, the other members of the band to catch up with. And as time presses on, day getting closer to night, he knows that he must accomplish these tasks before the evening begins and there's more football to watch or it's time to go out drinking again.

He's easily the most articulate of the three members, and this means not only that he writes the lion's share of the lyrics but also that he fights his corner the hardest in the band's arguments, which are constant, and often bitterly disputed. It's said that Shara Nelson left because, as much as anything, she couldn't bear arguing with him any more. After Massive Attack signed to Virgin, and Wild Bunch member Claude Williams had been relegated to a role as the band's driver, the Mitsubishi Shogun jeep that they bought with their advance was mysteriously crashed into the shop window of the Montpelier estate agents below Delge's first-floor flat.

He is also probably the nearest thing to a genius that the band has, and though he's the least musical of the three, his taste is good, his eye for detail extraordinary, and his interest in taking care of business sufficient to make up for the other two's love of laissez-faire. He began as a graffiti artist with a Robert De Niro fixation, spraying remarkably finished-looking pieces on to illegal sites, earning him two arrests, one where the paper pattern for a De Niro *Taxi Driver* mural was still in his hand as the police captured him. He was one of Britain's first, and most notable graffitists, forming part of an Anglo-American group with Wolverhampton's Goldie, now the star of drum and bass music, and who, like Tricky before him, and Bristol DJ Dom T before that, has also been a consort of Björk.

The son of a Bristol-Italian publican and an English mother, he has the small-businessman's concern for pounds and pence and takes on the role of general fixer for the band, as well as starting and finishing most of their arguments. He grew up in St Andrews, the same lower middle-class suburb as Mark Stewart just up the hill from St Paul's, and went to Monk's Park Comprehensive school, where he started in the sixth form until he was chucked out. I interviewed him at the pub around the corner from his house one evening, when all productive work had been abandoned for the night.

DELGE

During *Blue Lines* I thought I was going to have a heart attack. The only thing that saved me was because I thought I was too young. I was getting pins and needles in my hands with the arguments we had, and Cameron as a manager encouraged it in terms of what we did. He's a nightmare; he's into himself, and Neneh, and he's got a side to him which is very manipulative and it brings out the worst in you, as it did in all of us. I got lots of flak from it because he would use me as a conduit; he'd tell me things first, and once someone does that you're fucked. When Shara walked out on us, I knew that before anyone and I had to tell the guys. It was like why? How come we don't know? And I hated that. I said I don't want to know first, but I suppose when I wake up in the morning I always want to phone people up, and sometimes it's the death of me, but I can't handle not being in the knowledge.

Every time we argue it never gets resolved. Even if we have an argument about something silly, you can guarantee that it opens up a whole hall of mirrors, a corridor of doors that'll open up one at a time, until you get to the bottom and there's a fight. Yeah, at the bottom there's a pair of boxing gloves and it's like 'Ding–Ding!' With three people it's a nightmare 'cos you get a two–on –one situation every time. Sometimes when just two of us go somewhere, whichever combination it is, it's a lot easier. With the three of us there's always a slight tension, and it remains in the studio, totally. Sometimes I dread going into the studio with G and Mush, I fucking hate it. I can imagine us going into the studio at separate times and putting it together later.

It's like marriage, and sometimes you panic, you think, 'Well we're starting a record company now, we're getting in deeper, your mother–in–law's here, she's living with us, and it's all going wrong'. You think 'Oh my God', now you got kids, or to be precise, we got kids, which is the label, and if we split we've got a massive legacy of problems and the kids get fucked around. I spend most of my time hassling the others. G and Mush are so fucking laid back about it. I could spend a week without seeing them and I'm panicking. It's a contrast, I go out and get completely fucked and then I wake up in the morning with a hang-over, panicking.

Talk to G and Mush and they'll probably tell you I'm the most selfish, get–your–own–way bastard, which to a certain extent is true. You have to have a vision to see an album through to its end, even if you don't know what the fuck your partner's going to make of it. I have to think the next album's going to have the feeling of this, whatever this may be, it's gonna be epic, it's gonna have a punk element, the lyrics are gonna do this, the artwork's gonna be like this, the video – all these fucking ideas. I'm always projecting ahead. In my own life, if I sit in bed at night, it goes two ways. If I've been up all night, I get to bed, I put a pair of earplugs in, put my hands over my eyes and pray that I'll go to sleep. Or if I go to bed early, I just lie there playing out all these options in my mind and I can't sleep. I make a million decisions in my head, run through a million problems: my flat's falling apart, I want to redecorate the bastard, I want to start training for Wembley (for a pop–team match played before the Coca–Cola cup final), but then I want to buy that new Brazilian striker for Napoli. It's all these visions and predictions of how my football team's gonna be next year and how my flat's gonna be – nothing important about how the world's gonna be, or are we gonna sort out the Labour government, just the trivial shit like the album.

I'm always driven. I can never relax, but I've always got this fucking fear as well. I'm a lazy bastard, I'm a person of contrasts because certain days I wake up and I sit in front of the stereo for an hour thinking I could do this forever, then I shit meself thinking I could fall into a trap. And I run the bath, get in and I'll run the hot water with my toes and I'll lie there for an hour, I can't get out of the bath. Lyric books are lying on the table and I'll think right, bit of toast, cup of tea, phones ring, and I'll check the teletext to see what it says on the football news. Then I go and get the papers, there's a million distractions, and then at the end of the day I panic! I go 'Fuck, I haven't done anything.'

I suppose the graffiti thing appealed to me because I'd never done anything with my artistic abilities and I'd always had my dad saying to me 'What are you going to do?' and 'What a waste' and all that stuff, because I was academically useless because I had no concentration span whatsoever. The graffiti thing was just the perfect outlet for me to do what I wanted; it was illegal, it was an extension of adolescent knocking off school, glue–sniffing and that kind of thing, and being creative and being a bit of a hero.

About that time I'd met Miles and Nellee through various people, they were socially quite legendary, quite trendy. At that time me and my mate Pat Morrison used to go up to

(OPPOSITE) Delge in front of his finished piece on a Clifton wall, with a copy of the working plan, and a view of the whole

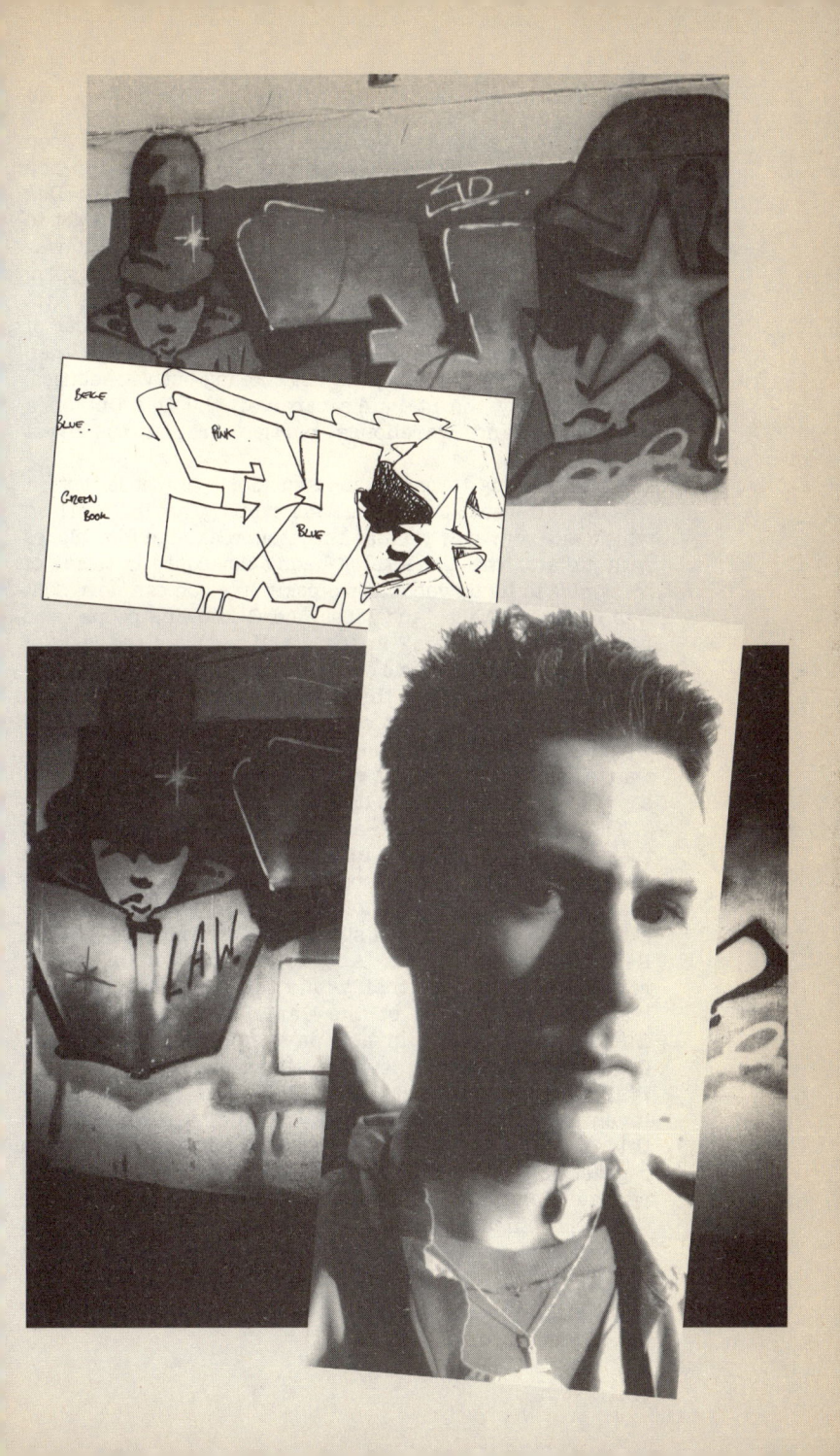

London to buy reggae twelves and I had quite a good collection of brand–new imports and all the early hip–hop stuff, really good shit, and cos G's the DJ down the Dug Out, and Dom and Milesy and everyone was there, I got to know them and to hang out and talk about music. It was new and it was exciting and the hip–hop thing was happening. Then the Wild Bunch started playing parties, the first thing was an illegal party on the downs in the summer of 1983. And the people who came to it loved it, and then there was warehouse parties, just booking out warehouses, and we'd play the St Paul's carnival, the Dug Out on a Wednesday and warehouse parties around the West Country.

As to starting to make our own music, in those days it was so different, the scene was run by an indie crowd which was very new wave, alternative rock, like four blokes with guitars. The dance thing hadn't developed in terms of being able to turn over music quickly like you can now, so it was a case of Nellee and Miles and G knowing people who had studios and getting in there and applying the logic of being a DJ, making music out of bits of other people's music and putting lyrics over the mike in a rap or reggae way, quite naive in an almost copycat way, same as any band would start. With every new rap record that came out it was, 'Have you heard that new rap record?' and everyone'd say 'Oh yeah, I'm going to do a rap like that.'

The DJs would go out and hunt for the same breaks they heard other DJs cut up in America or on records, all the classic breaks like 'Good Times', every DJ was doing that, every rapper was doing Sugarhill things and then getting into more modern stuff like Run DMC, Eric B and Rakim and Slick Rick. And of course you've got to remember during all that whole thing was the massive tradition in England of the Jamaican toasting scene. During those early hip–hop days you had Saxone and Coxsone and all those sound systems and Tipper Irie and Philip Levy and all those people and it was totally inventive poetically on the mike in that way. So all those things were happening together and I suppose the reggaethings were happening together and I suppose the reggae tinge and the dub tinge kept it English, or Caribbean English rather than being pure New York. And of course the break–dancers were breaking and graffiti

(OPPOSITE PAGE) The law's revenge: charge sheet for criminal damage, 1984

AVON AND SOMERSET CONSTABULARY

STATEMENT OF CHARGE(S)

Trevor Ross Police Station A Division

Surname	DELNAJA.
	Sex M
Other Name(s)	ROBERT
Date of Birth	21/1/65,
	Charge Sheet No. AT/2153/P
Address(es)	7, HOPE CHAPEL HILL,
	HOTWELLS.

You are charged with the offence(s) shown below. Do you wish to say anything? You are not obliged to say anything unless you wish to do so, but whatever you say will be taken down in writing and may be given in evidence

Charge No.

168
S.O. For that he on the 22nd August 1984, in the City of Bristol, Without lawful excuse damaged property belonging to Knightstone Housing Association namely a wall, amounting to £50.00p, intending to damage any such property or being reckless as to whether such property would be damaged.

Criminal Damage Act 1971, Section 1(1).

No REPLY

artists were copying the *Wild Style* moves. When *SUBWAY ART* came out that ended my interest in graffiti because eventually everyone had a sketchbook, everyone was an artist and the whole thing became so faddish and ridiculous that no one was doing what was the most important thing, which was painting illegally on the street, which was the exciting thing about it. In terms of being in the Wild Bunch, there was a million DJs around suddenly and a million rappers and though it didn't force you in the studio, it kind of nudged you along. There was so much copycat business that you wanted to do something to establish yourself as an individual again, and you couldn't do that in the same way as everyone else was doing, so being in the studio was something which had to be a progression.

The first thing we did was 'Tearing Down the Avenue', a demo we did in the studio. We went to Japan with it and did some recording there and did a tour which was quite a big thing because when we came back it meant that there was two choices. Nellee and Miles being more cosmopolitan than me and G and Claude at the time ('cos Mush was on the sidelines at the time, I suppose everyone was treating him as an apprentice DJ, although he'd hate me to say that, but that's how it was), they wanted to go to London, but the rest of us weren't ready for it. And when we came back I got chucked out of the clan. I missed my girlfriend and I came back and they threw me out. It was my first experience of touring and I didn't like it.

The Japan thing came about because of contacts in London, I think it was Bruce Smith who was in Rip Rig with Neneh and stuff, and he had a lot of contacts there. And when we came back Nellee and Miles decided it was time to go to London and the rest of us said no, we're staying here, being younger as well, and that was when the Island thing came about, 'cos they took the demos there. It was such a trendy scene and the Bristol–London connections were quite strong on that level. Neneh was starting to appear in terms of an artist and all that was going on, the whole *Face* thing, the Buffalo thing was large.

I stayed in Japan for about a month and the rest of the guys stayed for two. I just left. I left a note saying I couldn't take it anymore, basically, came back and I was gutted and I worked for the BBC for two months washing pots for

(OPPOSITE PAGE) Massive Attack before the release of *Protection* July 1994 (*photo*: Mondino)

Angela Rippon. Fucking nightmare. I had to wear little blue overalls and go to Kwik-Save and pick up frozen meat and stuff. It was almost like an exercise in self-*dis*esteem, where I'd walk up the road in this blue overall with a box of frozen food thinking, 'I was in Japan once, I was in a band', you know what I mean? And no one would believe me. I'd even talk about it at dinner, it had completely taken my character down. And then the boys came back from the tour and I was like, can I go in the band again, and they said well we like you, but we're never going to work with you again and I was in ruins, total ruins.

In Japan we played in clubs and some really pathetic fashion shows where we had radio mikes and we were dressed up as, like Coco the Milkman I suppose, fucking big clown boots and milkman's hats and big white coats with radio mikes – nonsense. We also went there with the expectation that we were going to be rich straight off and we were just blagging it on frozen pizzas and low-rent old apartments, having to squat in the shitters and wash yourself in a plastic bowl – it was like a nightmare. We had no cash, we were so skint that at eight in the evening we'd walk two miles to clubs where they'd let you in if you were European or American 'cos you were trendy and there'd be free food there and a free bar; basically our night out was actually to eat.

Nellee and Miles got themselves kitted out with top apartments 'cos that's the way they are, they're very resourceful, while I was living in this ski jacket with Asian flu, taking antibiotics, really having a miserable time. I said 'I'm out of here.' But the worst thing was, why I blew it, was that I went out shopping on the day I left and they wouldn't forgive me for that, 'cos I said 'I'm out of here but I've still got a few hours to go shopping,'and I left with a big bag of goodies. But as the plane landed at Heathrow I was thinking 'What have I done?'

When they came back Nellee and Miles went to London and got on with it and got involved in a lot more of that Japanese–London culture exchange. I was way out of it by then but they got this deal with Island and then I got this knock on the door and 'We want you back in', you know, to write lyrics. I'm not saying they're fickle or anything. So then we did this recording and put out 'The Look of Love', which really was Miles' idea, with Shara who was from Adrian Sherwood's posse, and also this rap 'Tearing Down the Avenue', which we had demoed before. Technically, for

English hip–hop, it was out there on its own, but Island put it out on import and it was just at the point where Eric B and Rakim was happening and Mica Paris was happening and there was no time spent on it at all. It was out and that was it, it was gone. And then we re–released 'The Look of Love' and did a track called 'Machine Gun' and a track called 'Friends and Countrymen'. It was alright but it didn't really happen, but out of that we met Cameron, and Mush started working on tour with Neneh as a DJ, and doing a bit of work on *Raw Like Sushi* and they asked me to write lyrics for 'Manchild', which I did and that worked out. During that process Cameron discovered what we were up to and said you guys should get in the studio, funded us and put us up at his place, got us a studio set up and put us in with John Sharp, who we nicknamed Johnny Dollar as a piss–take, who became the co–producer of *Blue Lines*. He was a programmer working for Cameron and they're still together as a team.

At this point Nellee and Miles were signatories to the Island deal but the rest of us weren't. I remember being sat in the kitchen with my dad working out how to put a contract together so I could make sure I got paid for my lyrics. I went out and got some Letraset and designed this 3D–headed notepaper and me and my dad wrote a letter and Nellee said 'What's this bollocks?', and I said, 'So I make sure I get paid something for this record,' and I got about five hundred pounds sent through the post, and at that time I was chuffed, but at that point they were the Wild Bunch and we were just hanging out in the background providing the flavours.

And then Miles went to live in America, he disappeared and went to Japan, got married there and now he lives in New York with a couple of kids. So he was out of the picture and Nellee was by then firmly entrenched with Soul to Soul and they were large, and Nellee was large and so Cameron put the rest of us in the studio and off we went. Some of it was bravado, some of it was bullshit, we didn't know what we were doing but we had ideas and a lot of them were based in the past still. And I got together with Tricky at that point. The earliest memory of Trick I've got, I remember meeting him and we did this jam at Trinity and I was on the mike doing this live version of 'Tearing Down the Avenue' and there was Tricky at the front, giving it 'Yes!'. He was working with the Fresh Four and we kept up a bit of a relationship. And no matter what Tricky says about him being the best songwriter in the world and a genius I can remember that his lyrics were basically, even on *Blue Lines*, 'I'm a tricky kid, I did this, I do that, I'm a tricky kid'; and I was saying no, why don't we do something a bit different, get a bit more out there, bit more abstract, start using different words. I'm not saying it's me me me, but I was saying let's use the quiet voices; the whispered rap was something I was really into. And we'd demoed a few things with Steve Haley, a mate of ours. We started recording in his house with instrumentals on tape, and a Wally Badarou track which later became 'Daydreaming', and he got out this really good plate mike, one of those little ambient pick-up mikes and we did it directly into that which gave it the quality that we wanted, which was that close-up-in-your-face whisper, like right in your ear.

The way *Blue Lines* was put together was so hit-and-miss. Cameron was there directing the music and Neneh was there helping us, with 'The Big Wheel' which we wrote for Horace Andy, and I wrote with Neneh. Mushroom would be on the turntables cutting up some crazy beat and Shara just started singing this song which she called 'Kiss and Tell' (which became 'Unfinished Sympathy'), which was not really happening, but there was a vibe to it and Johnny started playing this keyboard live and suddenly we put it together on tape. The next day we're chatting about it and fucking hell, there's something there. It was a general consensus of opinion, let's get it sorted out, but none of us were in a position of scoring out a classical orchestra, so Johnny got in his mate and there it was. And then it was really down to arranging the song, piecing it together like a jigsaw, with loads of bits missing, which is what gives it the space. It's like you take the bits apart, find the accidents in it and then deliberate with them.

'Five Man Army' is a total system echo, it's like here's the instrumental, here's the bass line, everyone take it in turns, which was very freestyle. We all did a bit each, we all had our lyrics so we got in the studio and did it. 'Turbo turbo' was a lyric Grant had going back about ten years ago, and he's been struggling to come up with anything ever since, and you can quote me on that. The bass line was from a thing called 'Five Man Army', a reggae tune. The gutting thing about it was that before we did the deal with Cameron we were working on a demo and Cameron said Soul to Soul were getting a label together so we went into the studio with them and Jazzy was like King Midas you know, with the cane and that, and we played him these demos and when their second album came out it had that 'Five Man Army' bass line of one of the tracks. We were fucking livid but Nellee was like, we don't know anything about it. Those were the days when DJs were covering up the labels on the records, blanking the labels so no one could tell what they were playing, all that sort of shit. It's like Mush turns up with a beat and he won't tell you where it's from.

The *Blue Lines* recording dragged on and on because of our disorganization which we still maintain, because we're like that and we're lazy bastards, and 'cos Cameron was working with Neneh and lots of different things. It took much longer than it should have, in work terms I think it took about six months. It's quite embarrassing when you talk about it as a seminal album because it was just born out of chaos and there were so many collaborators on it. But the thing I like about it is that after that album, after the credit, all the people who worked on it said 'Oh, they didn't do fuck all, it was down to Shara or Cameron or Johnny, it weren't down to Massive Attack at all'; and they all went off and did their own thing, and it didn't happen. A lot of things are born out of collaboration, whether it's a band with a singer or whether it's between two people like Nellee and Jazzie, and once you separate the two you just lose the half of it. Shara was really weird about it at the end when she fell out with us. Her vibe was that we ripped her off but basically she got a manager in, out of the blue and when that happens everything changes; you get the whisper in the ear, 'Hey love, you could be doing this, they're taking the piss out of you.' It was also misunderstanding the music business, which we were trying to get our heads around. It's all well and good getting a big advance and spending it and wasting it on cars which then get crashed six months later and all that shit. We did all that: giving money to your mates, building studios which never got finished, you lose it all immediately. We were paying Shara a retainer but not on a basis of recoupment, so we were taking money off Virgin which we had to recoup and we weren't getting paid. In fact we still haven't recouped on *Blue Lines* 'cos it cost so much to market, but Shara and all these other collaborators were getting paid from day one, they were getting royalties for every record sold whereas we were still living off the advance.

Sometimes you want a permanent singer, sometimes you want to work without one. If we had a permanent singer with us all the time we could really work with them and develop ideas of songs and that would make the writing process a lot easier 'cos often I find myself writing lyrics, when we're putting music together, without even an idea of how the melody of the song might work with it, and it's all abstracted. But in some ways that's maybe how we get the feel of what we do. There's always this big space between the moments of getting it finished and bringing people in, and the space between creates the tension in the songs. The fact that you have to have strangers involved, means you get these things where you have to work out deals on the spot with people – I want two points, I want fifty per cent – and there's all that tension as well which you're supposed to get management to do. It spills over into the studio, and this is a good thing and a bad thing, because you get the tension which is interesting, but you get the net result which is bollocks, but the thing we've never done is to be held to ransom over it. People have said Massive Attack are the best diving board in the business, everyone that's gone off it – Shara, Nicolette, Tricky, even Tracey Thorn with the rebirth of Everything But The Girl, have done well out of it.

With my lyrics, my ideas are based on fragments, the title's one fragment and the rest of the songs don't necessarily add up to make the whole broken mirror but you can put them together in whatever order you like because it's like – the best way of describing it is like travelling through a crowded bar and stopping for a few moments at each conversation and listening to bits and pieces and at the end of it you create a summary of what the place was like, but made up of so many different parts. There's definitely room to make up things that don't make sense to yourself, but they have rhythmic value and atmospheric value. It's like the Beatles' 'Come Together'. I'd sit there with my sister and we'd sing it, and we'd both know what we were talking about, but it didn't actually mean anything. That way of writing has always stuck with me and I love it.

Blue Lines did big in sales, it charted at twelve and when I said that to my mum she said 'What, in the real chart?' It was unreal and all this stuff was going off around us. The praise was ridiculous but the lasting praise, like when you see it as dance album of the decade or top five album of the decade, and you look at the things behind it you go, no way, that was brilliant, you know what I mean? We thought about it a lot, in terms of individual things in the studio, arrangements and sequencing of tracks. I do take a large role in that because I'm so fussy, G'll tell you. I'm a selfish cunt, whereas on the pre–production programming level I take a back seat and let Mush get on with it, unless it's a vision track where you think, 'I want it to sound like this with this bass line.' If it's a case of a section of music that has to be built up then Mush'll get in there, if it's a dub or a bass loop then G'll get in there. Me, I'll sit back. We did the sequence of tracks by trial and error, by track time and memory, like you can't put that there, you've got two Horaces and a Shara. It's almost like doing the lottery.

When we'd finished we did think it was good, yeah. There was stuff on it I hated and I always will hate; I hate the track 'Blue Lines' and I don't like 'Be Thankful', it's a nice track but I don't like it; I don't like 'Lately' very much. My favourite tracks are 'Safe From Harm', 'The Big Wheel', 'Unfinished Sympathy', 'Daydreaming' and 'One Love'. I love those tracks but the rest can go. I'd find it so easy to make a compilation of *Blue Lines* and *Protection*, I'd know exactly what'd go on, 'cos I hate half the tracks on both albums, quite simply.

When it came to doing live stuff, with *Top of the Pops* and stuff, Shara's point of view was 'Oh, they made me get up and do it on my own', which was wrong because she loved it, being the centre of attention, like anyone would. Our point of view was that we had to swallow a bit because we wanted to do the best for the song and represent it on television; 'You've got a great voice and you don't need to see us hanging around saying we're the band'. But in a way you're gutted, you're not there; it's *Top of the Pops* and your mum's going 'Where are you?' It's our song but it made for a situation where everyone said Shara's the lead singer. We didn't have a plan to play live, as far as we were concerned we were lucky enough to make an album. We didn't have a five–year plan and we weren't a band. It's only now that we've got into what we're doing that we realize we've got something to offer.

The first American tour was a fucking nightmare, man. We had the curtain at Prince's club, Glam Slam, in Minneapolis before the encore; one minute you're on the mike and then this big tumbling piece of velvet comes down out of the sky. I always had this vision of Prince sitting there on a throne in a VIP room, with the thumbs down like the gladiators, and then some guy taking the nod ... It was like we were trapped on the wrong side of the curtain like Morecambe and Wise. I remember I said, 'Let's take the beer on stage', because we had two turntables, six geezers all taking it in turns to pick up the mike, no set, just a bare stage with nothing to hide behind, so what do you do between songs? You just dance around pretending you're having fun at the party. So we started off with one beer during the set, then somebody donated some more and we had a whole crate on stage and we were going fag, beer, fag, beer, just to keep yourself occupied. I remember me and Tricky both trying to push each other out the door first on to the stage, like 'You're on lads', and me and Tricky spinning around in the door in front of everyone, going 'No! No!, I'm not going on first!'

Someone just said you'd better go to America with the sound system. Fucking joke! No one understood it. We got some polite applause and we did a couple of shows where it was quite alright. In Chicago we played downstairs in this basement and upstairs was the Buzzcocks and we met them and they said, 'You guys are really brave doing what you're doing.' After the Prince gig Cameron phoned up and he said he was pulling us out. Of course, I was the first one to know again. And it was knee-deep in snow and it was, 'Oh my God, we've done the worst part of the tour', we just had one gig left in Washington and then we were going to the West Coast and it was the one bit we were looking forward to, but no, no, you gotta come back home. It was like a nightmare.

No one understood us over there. They had no handle on our ironic humour and we were doing radio interviews and there's like these big silences and it was all going wrong. We were down in Boston and we don't get on with the girl, the rep, and she keeps staring at Tricky and being really patronizing and going, 'You're cute aren't you?' and Tricky's going, 'What the fuck are you looking at?', so we hate her from the first moment on, and she takes us to this radio station and we get there and no one's told us he's the most important DJ on the East Coast. He's massive, he breaks records, he's influential and he interviews us and though we're not trying to be awkward, he's saying why do you do your music. Because we like it,

we say. But there must be some reason, he says. So I says
what would Aaron Neville say to that, and he says, 'Aaron
Neville's a personal friend of mine', so I said, 'Alright
Marky Mark, look at that bollocks', and it was 'Marky
Mark's a personal friend of mine.' On the way out of the
interview he shakes my hand and says, 'You guys are
going to be really big in America', nice one, and then when
we get back to the hotel there's a call from Cameron saying
Sunny Joe says they should drop you right away. He
phones up the record company and says drop that band.
Everything was going mental but we just waltzed through
doing our sound–system show, turning out a load of
bollocks but we think it's great.

When we came back, it was the whole thing with
Cameron. We weren't happy and we were basically finishing with him, we were just falling to bits over a million
things. We fell out with Cameron and we fell out with each
other for a long time. There was all kinds of stuff going
on. We were doing Jack shit and Cameron suddenly said,
'You guys better start your new album', and we went up
to Virgin and signed the second committal deal for the
album, and the fact is he got his commission, took his
percentage and was gone. We had no manager, no
co–producer (since Johnny Dollar had left with Cameron,
when he left the country with his tax problems). Shara
had gone, Horace was in Jamaica where he lives. Me and
Tricky were living together which was bizarre because we
were meant to be writing together but we just used to go
out and get pissed or did fuck all, and so that was that.
There was nothing going on, we just had to do our own
thing, getting your own spirit together, trying to excite
yourself with your own ideas. And if you couldn't do that
there was nothing there, no framework, no studio and the
only thing was that EMI were taking over Virgin so we
weren't under a lot of pressure. They were cutting their
roster down and we didn't even know we'd been dropped
until we phoned up our A&R man.

It's funny how people change. Interviewers say, 'Oh you
guys are finished, one–hit–wonders' and you start to
believe it yourself. And we spent the whole time writing
music, writing lyrics, getting ideas together and Tricky
was doing his thing, and then me and Tricky fell out,
which was a really sad thing in a way. He's doing his
thing, I'm doing mine, we're both happy. But it was weird
because we were paying Tricky a wage because he didn't

have any money, but we're not standing to get any of it back on the basis of writing together. So Tricky's going off writing but he's writing on his own and then turning round and saying 'I've got this tune, you should do it on your album', and we said, 'Well what the fuck's it got to do with us? You don't want us to fuck with it, it's your tune.' So he says 'I think it's out of order', and I'm saying 'What about the shit we're supposed to be doing?' And it really pissed me off when he said in the press that I was trying to hold him back. It was bollocks. I was there every day trying to get him out of bed saying right, let's work. So he moved out because it was a nightmare living together, it was hard enough to get into the same room.

All of us felt aggrieved because we were paying someone to do nothing, 'cos our money was going down, our budget was fucked, we'd crashed our Shogun jeep. And we'd spent about twenty–five grand on equipment, and you can't sell it again, and we're paying to keep Shara and Horace going, which is fair enough. At the time it's a good idea, it's not business sense but it's a good idea 'cos what we were dealing with was a family thing of keeping everyone together, but at the end of the day there's no return on it and when your money runs out you're gone. With me and Tricky not writing together it brought about bad feeling, but in the end it's worked out great: you got a great Tricky album, you've got a great recording artist, and we're doing our thing as well. But at the time it felt like both things were cancelling each other out. But it's like the Man United side the other night, they've lost a lot of payers but it's still a young side and it's still doing it.

On *Protection* there was a big gap. We all went off in our own ways and we worked with different people, I worked with the Insects and Tricky on a couple of things. In a way we're a most unorthodox band because I don't like sitting in a room with G and Mush putting my lyrics across the mike. I feel self–conscious and I always feel they're going to be hypercritical and stop me with 'What you trying to do? You sounded stupid there.' I'd rather do it on my own or with someone else and then bring them in and say check this out. And Mush works in the same way, he's very conscious of detail and he'll sit for three hours working out a hi–hat sound. To the rest of the people in the studio it's a complete wind–up, it's the most annoying thing in the world, but to him he's got an idea and it's always worth it. So in *Protection* we did a lot of going our own ways and then of course we got together with Nellee and Marius (Marius De Vries, credited with programming) and sometimes we left the studio and let them get on with it, to give them space, because sometimes you need to give the person who's mixing it a chance.

Mushroom

Some people get the impression that Mushroom isn't all there. He has a distant, abstracted air to him, especially compared to the quick wit and easy piss-taking of Del Naja and Marshall. Conversation can go on around him and he seems to be oblivious to it until suddenly he comes alive and makes a contribution that picks up on something that happened ten minutes ago. But his still waters run deep. He's the real hip-hop heart and soul of the group, his seriousness and dedication to the beats what impressed the other members of the Wild Bunch when he was just a kid hanging around. On stage he undergoes a transformation, and as a DJ he can be remarkably theatrical, spinning round with a record in each arm, expertly manipulating the decks with a ridiculous ease, cueing up tracks and cutting them up in a blur of movement.

Years ago, I taught GCSE Film Studies to him at college, where his interests in zombie movies and splatter flicks weren't much acknowledged by the official syllabus. He was an unusually serious student, though, who had paid his own fees after time out from education working in a restaurant, from where, probably, his nickname derives, as it certainly isn't anything to do with drugs.

MUSHROOM

The whole thing really started from when I was at school, when I was fifteen or so. I was at St George Comprehensive, which at the time wasn't a very nice place. There was a lot of racism and St George was like on a borderline between St Paul's and Barton Hill and you'd get all the white skinheads and psychobillies plus all the black guys from St Paul's. The police riot vans used to be outside the school with dogs every night because Barton Hill was full of NF skinheads at the time. I first heard hip–hop from this guy's car outside the school and I just checked it out straight away, went and bought the music and that was that. I met G at the record shop, Revolver, where he was working. I saw all these Wild Bunch stickers there and so I said to G, 'Who are the Wild Bunch?', and he said 'I am the Wild Bunch', and it just snowballed from there.

They were playing all over the place and I used to follow them, going to all the hip–hop jams, up in London and at the Dug Out, and all the jams in Bristol. The Dug Out was a bit of a problem because I was only fifteen at the time but G sorted me out with a membership card so I wouldn't get hassled on the door. I started to try mixing straight away, as soon as I came out of school and began buying records. 3PM (an early Bristol mixing crew) were part of it as well, especially Krissy Kriss 'cos he goes back with me a long way, he was the guy who I grew up with and we started doing the stuff with a couple of decks. We used to get together with our records and we made slip mats out of greaseproof paper because we couldn't fathom out what you'd use or where you'd get them from as they were so obscure at the time. You'd get little globules of grease on the records and have to try and scrape them off ....

I didn't know what to do when I left school so I thought I'd be a chef and I got a YTS job at Michael's restaurant. Meanwhile, we formed a crew, and did little things ourselves. There were loads of crews around at the time, like 2 Bad, who were Dom T and Ed Sargent, who were on a par with the Wild Bunch at the time, but they wouldn't cut it up so much, they were smoother. I knew the Wild Bunch and I would just be hanging around and chilling with them when they had their sets and when they weren't practising I'd mess around with their turntables, and they'd just say 'yeah'. They were all like ten years older than me and it was really funny just to sit on a crate and watch these adult guys organize their stuff, like watch them sort the money out after a gig in Gloucester; there were arguments with promoters, they had to organize the coaches and I just used to watch it all go on ...

There'd be fierce arguments between them. Everyone was so different from each other and that's what the arguments came from. I've got to be careful here, about

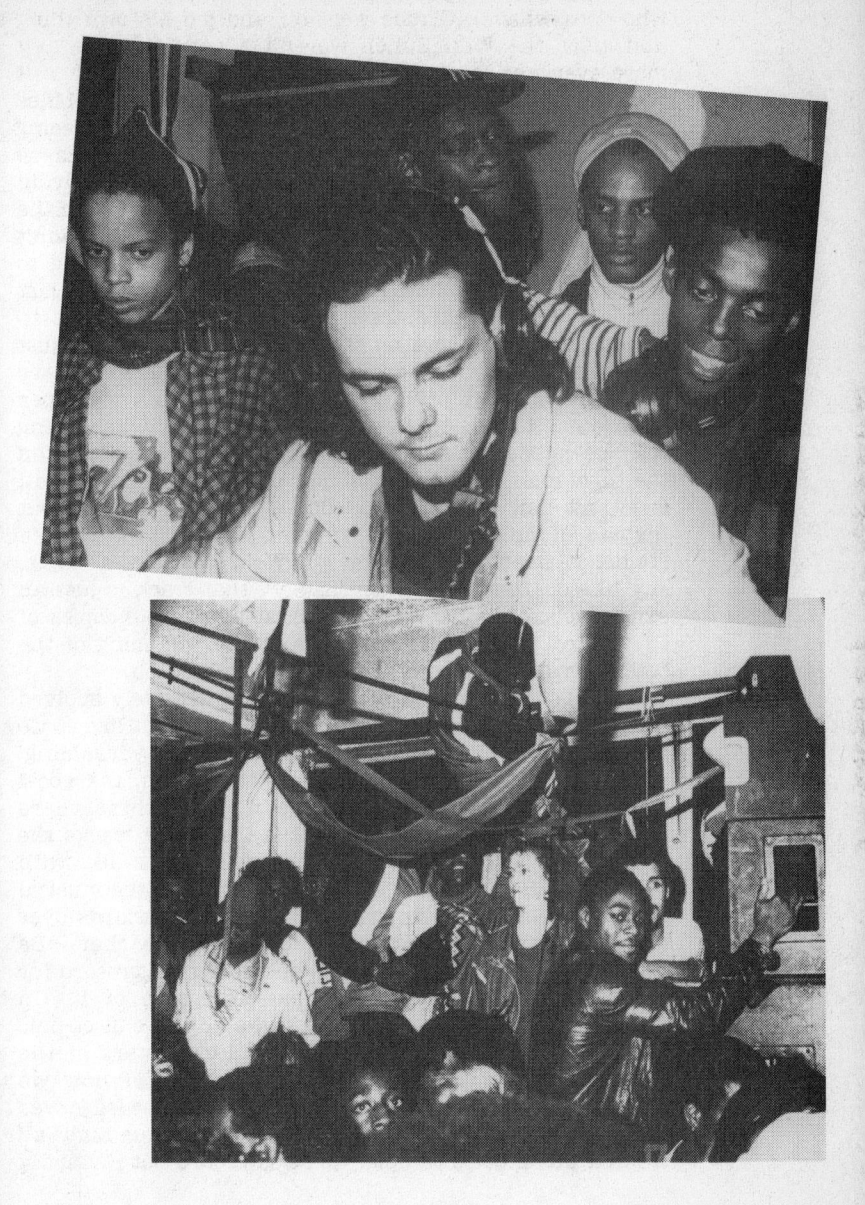

The Redhouse jam: *above* with Mushroom left and Nellee Hooper front

who does what ... Claude went off and did his own thing
and after the Wild Bunch weren't a conglomerate any
more everyone went off and did their own thing. When it
came to the recordings, that was more Nellee and Miles
because Miles had some really strong ideas about piecing
things together. In those days it was really hard because
engineers didn't know what you wanted and it's only in
the last few years that this country has taken off with the
knowledge of this music; samples and stuff they hadn't
heard of. I remember going into a studio and trying to
explain to this guy how I wanted this drum break to last
throughout the whole track, so I needed two tracks to
record on – there were no samples – but the engineer just
couldn't get his head around it. The early tracks were
done with drum machines and sampling drum machines
but looping breaks wasn't really around. The whole thing
that we've been doing is making music from the decks, on
the turntables, but making a new piece of music out of it;
it wasn't new to us, it was doing what we did live but
instead of mixing at a jam, being able to tape it in a
studio. It wasn't much different. We'd just take a break,
say like on *Blue Lines* with 'Lately', that track is just an
exact replica of what would go on at a jam, two copies of
the record cut up, just the break at the beginning of the
track or whatever, with a vocal put over the top.

On *Blue Lines* a lot of the tracks were definitely evolved
from our camp, the root of the idea of things like 'Safe
From Harm', 'Lately', 'Five Man Army'. 'Daydreaming'
was actually recorded years before the album, the vocal
was done at Steve Haley's, something like three years
before, on a plate mike. But with a lot of the tracks the
root of the idea had been in our heads for ages, like with
'Safe From Harm'. I had the loop and through the musical
inserts of Johnny Dollar we put bass and keyboards over
the top, but the idea was around years earlier. 'Be
Thankful' – that was G's record, he'd loved that record for
years and he just wanted to do a version of it. On
Protection it wasn't like that. We had a bit more electronic
knowledge and that played a much larger part in the
music, took it away really from the basis of how we
started, made it more technical, but the old knowledge was
still there and it's still a hip–hop album. On *Blue Lines* all
we had was a basic sampler and a keyboard but I actually

(OPPOSITE) New York's Fearless 4 play St Paul's, with Peso on the decks.

enjoyed the making of that album more. It was more of what we were about, what the Wild Bunch and stuff was about, it came from the seeds of that ... With *Protection* we almost disappeared up our own electronic passageways, even though it's still got that rough sound to it, which is from the old knowledge.

For me the Americanness of hip–hop was no problem. As soon as I left school I went straight to America. I said I've got to go where this is going on, and my dad's a New Yorker as well, even though I've never really seen him. So I went to America in about 1985 and ever since I've been going there. We did a jam in Bristol with the Fearless Four from New York and I hooked up with one of them, Peso. Krissy Kriss had family over there, and Peso had said come on over and I did. I went over with Kriss and stayed with his family for a bit and then stayed with Peso in Brooklyn for quite a time. It was funny because that was a mad time in music, you had some mad revolutionary armies coming out around you like Schooly D, so to go to see that we'd go to the jams. In the black community that was all there was at that time, that was their roots. We were staying in the projects and stuff and that was all there was.

I'm still into the thing of the sound system, but that's where I'm coming from. I've only lived through this type of music, hip–hop or whatever. I'm still deep within that groove, but obviously, for certain reasons, you've got to evolve it into a live band. G was a reggae DJ before the Wild Bunch so reggae has always been his music. D was a punk before so he likes those types of thrashy influences. Life really begins after you leave school doesn't it? That's when you begin to leave the dictatorship of school and start to do your own thing, which is funny really because hip–hop is an actual tree that has grown from nothing and is still here. It's not like you can go back, it's within our generation and there are kids now who have been born into it and are now making millions out of it, which is mad. There's kids now who when they talk about the old school, they're meaning things like Eric B and Rakim, which was miles on for us.

TRICKY

From the Tricky Kid of *Blue Lines*, sounding very effectively like a little artful dodger ('getting a Visa card nowadays isn't hard') in that deadpan, *faux-naif*, childish voice, with an audio-persona like some classic-English comedy stooge from a Carry On movie or Charlie Drake's *The Worker*, nothing quite prepares you for the decadent, world-weary old roué of his debut album *Maxinquaye* released in early 1995. Except, perhaps, a track recorded in 1991 with Geoff Barrow, later of Portishead, entitled 'Nothing's Clear' and released on a Bristol charity album called *The Hard Sell*. Against a repeated piano figure sampled from the *Betty Blue* soundtrack (and perhaps itself a sample from the South-African pianist Abdullah Ibrahim), and the interjection of stabbing horns stolen from the Specials, the familiar *Blue Lines* voice talks as quietly as a voice on a record can, of this and that, wondering what's going on in his life, because nothing's clear.

It's a stunningly alienated track, the still small-boy's voice towered over by the shadowy heights of menacing riffs, with the perfect circle of the little piano motif representing the still centre of the singer's dream world, reassuring, condolent, maternal. This tricky kid, it's evident, is a troubled soul, or at least the text of the music invites you to make such inferences, rather than, for example, inviting you to dance, for this isn't hip-hop as we know it, or knew it then. It's self-aware, tortuous, the lyrics deliberately foregrounding the singer's unease and vulnerability, celebrating them

even. 'How things are' he says, 'together will destroy; then we can destroy what we are; together we'll build what we are, when we dream the spirit free.'

Maxinquaye

From here, rather than from *Blue Lines* (on which Tricky was known as Massive Attack's YTS member, being paid a retainer of twenty-five pounds a week), the remaining distance to the album, with the singles 'Aftermath' and 'Ponderosa' as stations on the way, isn't too far, but it's still a hell of a journey. The sound world of the singles and the album is twisted, rough and crusty, an equivalent to the blasted surfaces and terminal run–down–ness of *Blade Runner*, everyone's favourite entropic text. Even the jerky, half-familiar loops of the samples sound as if they can barely sustain themselves, as if the batteries playing them are running down, the speed wavering, the whole engine about to judder to a halt, a last quivering beat struggling to pulse out its remaining filament of energy, like a chicken with its head cut off, before it keels over and dies.

The music of Tricky can make you write like that, and with *Maxinquaye* (named for his dead mother) it did, as the press rolled over and tickled its own belly with all the projected alienation and fin-de-siècle angst that the accumulated disgust from years of re-viewing bad music by worse bands can give you. Tricky struck a chord and everyone who reviewed the record thought they owned the music themselves, that it was their fear and confusion it was expressing, and that the personal had been made universal, bad emotions and bad sex recollected in tranquillity. That the guiding sensibility of the age actually belonged to a dysfunctional young man from a council estate

Massive Attack's Tricky kid. He was known as the group's YTS member, receiving a retainer of £25 a week.

didn't invalidate the experience. On the contrary, it made it even more piquant. And when he spoke of darkness, of twisted eroticism, of fucking you up the ass just for a laugh (even worse, getting Martina to sing it), it merely reinforced the sense that here was a figure who had answered the call for some new, more visceral, form of expression for an age where rubber wear had permeated the high-street shops and bondage fiction invaded the traditional Mills and Boon market. The jagged, disconnected, rumbling imagery of the lyrics also removed the album from the familiar tropes of hip-hop, even in the English version pioneered by Massive Attack, and the voice of the singer Martina – rather overlooked at the time but now seeming absolutely crucial – added a nicely judged layer of gloss (well, glossy compared to Tricky anyway) to the pitted surface of the tunes. Whatever, the Tricky of *Maxinquaye* was a long way from 'Maggie this, Maggie that, Maggie means inflation', on *Blue Lines*.

If anyone was to put together words like this it should have been Robert Del Naja of Massive Attack. He read the books, saw the films, talked to people in the know and could, if pressed, refer to the cut ups of William Burroughs when asked to sing for his supper. But coming from Tricky it was as if he was talking in a language he didn't fully understand, like the poet Chatterton making up the diction of an imaginary fourteenth-century poet out of bits of antique prose found in an old manuscript box.

The album, of course, also predicted its own success by cannily appropriating the sounds of hip-hop's traditional enemy, the guitar, and by so removing itself from the normal agenda of dance music that it had to appeal to navel-gazing rock fans. This was hip-hop you could get depressed to, stare at the bedroom wall to, write suicide notes or poetry to. Even goths could love it, if there were any left. And the selling of the album cannily maximized *Maxinquaye*'s cross-genre potential by cloaking the artist and his muse, Martina, in gender-bending mufti for publicity shots, the Island art department making good use of the corporate dressing-up box, Rocky Horror make-up and enough rope for the two of them to hang themselves with. Tricky's distinctive, sallow, drugged-up face was painted and preened, with a *Clockwork-Orange* false eyelash here, a smear of lipstick there, and his skinny body dressed in drag, while Martina was made to be the groom to his bride in the celebrated wedding shots. Here was the artist in a dress, the same man who had dissed Prince to girls in Bristol clubs as being unmanly. 'I've always worn dresses', said Tricks to the press. 'Bollocks' said the Bristol posse, who knew him as a macho would-be bad boy from way back.

Knowle West

If in Bristol people had generally been amazed that Massive Attack had managed to come up with *Blue Lines*, they had to be dumbfounded by what came out of Tricky. He was the stoned kid who was at every party, every club, always out of it but usually cheery and good-natured; he was the one always trying to chat up the young Clifton girls and get his wicked way with them. He had been a fixture at all the scenes, usually arriving very late and very intoxicated, for years.

Some of his new *gravitas* must have come from the influence of the Wild Bunch and Massive connections, who revered the films of Scorsese and especially *Taxi Driver* and *GoodFellas*, for their violence as much as anything, and who were connoisseurs of splatter movies and zombie flicks, the kind of film buffs who continuously rewind the video to replay the scene in *Scarface* where Al Pacino is cutting the baddie's legs off with a chainsaw. But that was only the half of it, if that. Some of what went into Tricky, and came back out again the other end as art, was, of course, down to the traditional Bristol-posse sport of blagging, of trying to speak a language of whose vocabulary or grammar he had only a rudimentary command. But some of it, and perhaps an awful lot, had to come from what really was him, from his background and from the kind of alienation that you don't get much of in Camus or Sartre, the kind that comes from the school of hard knocks.

Knowle West is an unlovely suburb in the south of Bristol, a council estate with a frightening reputation these days for heroin abuse amongst its young residents, which has prompted a group of mothers on the estate to start their own action group, getting funding for a centre and wielding enough political clout to make ministers come down and survey the damaged lives their sons and daughters are living. It's also the estate with the worst record of racial problems – or problems if you're not white – in the city, with black, Asian and mixed-race families who have been rehoused there often bailing out as soon as possible to move to even worse accommodation where the hassles aren't so bad. Commendably, the city council has tried to punish the racists by attempting to get them rather than their victims chucked out but it's a difficult policy to put into action, and one with calamitous consequences for the family that gets to stay among the neighbours of the racists forced to depart. Knowle West is far enough from the centre of the city for it to remain a more or less enclosed environment. You can't just walk up the road to the centre or Park Street, and in the neighbouring areas, Knowle, Bedminster, Totterdown, Brislington, there's nothing much happening.

Tricky, Adrian Thaws as was, was born and grew up here with the added disadvantage of a mum who died when he was four, and an absent father who flew the coop before that. 'After that I was passed around between relatives in different parts of Bristol and I didn't see my father again until I was twelve', he has said. He was brought up by his uncle's family and by his nan, who listened to Billie Holiday and Nina

Simone records ('rocking in my area, rocking on the balcony, my baby just cares for me, that's funny'), and he had to endure the added misfortune of having both asthma and eczema, the former meaning that he missed a lot of school, the latter giving his skin a layer of distress. Sometimes his nan let him off school deliberately, so he could sleep late in the morning and spend the days in her company, the cherished, over-protected child of an old woman.

'I went to school with him', recalls Flynn, of the Bristol drum and bass team Flynn and Flora. 'Well, when he was at school, that is. He was a really bad asthmatic and a lot of the time he just used to get taken out. I was asthmatic as well and that's how we knew each other at school. We'd both have inhalers and pills to take, but he really used to get taken pretty badly and had to go to hospital. We went to Knowle Juniors and Merrywood Boys together but he was always in and out of school. He was always adventurous and different, always one step ahead of what was going on and he got us into a lot of things, breaking or hip-hop or whatever, saying you've got to check this out. His cousin used to go out with Claude from the Wild Bunch so he used to get tapes and know what was going on.' 'He was always coming in my brother's caff', remembers Flora 'and saying lyrics in your ear, and you'd say "that sounds crazy Tricks", but he was coming out with words that sounded so wicked, even then, because he's got such a nice voice and when he says something, it means something, it wasn't just a load of crap.' 'Tricky?', says Flynn's brother Krust, now another drum and bass producer. 'He was just Tricky, from way back.'

Tricky's level of juvenile delinquency was sufficiently developed for him to be arrested, the first time for robbing a YMCA games machine ('I stayed there and carried on playing the machines', he remembers, 'and then the police turned up'). He was also put in prison for four days when he was seventeen for passing forged notes. His asthma inhaler was taken off him and when he was attacked in his cell on the second night he rang the alarm button but no one answered. 'I was nearly dead', he remembered. 'That fucked me up completely.'

Despite whatever privations he suffered, he looks back at the experience of growing up with fondness, or at least he does when in a sunny mood, which was when I talked to him, at the time of the release of his first album. 'It was great fun', he said. 'A lot of my funniest times are from those days, hanging around with groups of kids having posse fights, nicking from off-licences and throwing a rocket at someone's car. We used to play this game where there'd be six of us, and one would lay on the floor and we'd pretend to kick them. After a while someone would come along and decide to be a hero and tell us to stop.' He progressed to mixing between gangs of white and black boys. 'I would hang around with a posse of pure black guys, and then with a posse of beer guys, all white; you've got to play both sides of the game, to have a few personalities so you can talk and chill with anybody. Both of them are still in me: the white guy making black music and the black guy making white music – it was all integrated from way back.'

Merrywood, his secondary school, a boys' comprehensive, was largely, though not overwhelmingly, attended by white pupils. In fact, unlike London, in Bristol there isn't a secondary school for any of the areas with the largest numbers of black residents, and black children attend a variety of institutions, all of them predominantly white, like Fairfield in Montpelier, Cotham Grammar, Monk's Park in Horfield (where Del Naja and Roni Size went) or Whitefields in Fishponds. Similarly, though St Paul's is renowned as the 'black' area of the city, it's not where most black people live. The inevitable integration of races in the schools and elsewhere is reflected in the music of the Bristol sound.

As Flynn says: 'You'd expect a lot of the Bristol-sound people to be from St Paul's but apart from Ray Mighty they're not. It's like coming from Knowle, and you get something from that. Other people, especially from London, see hip-hop as very defined, like it's one thing, 'this, this and this', but the people who don't see it as one thing tend to come from different areas and they're a little bit more open-minded when it comes to doing tracks. People from Bristol, who aren't from where you expect them to be from, go "use that, and use that", and they're much more open. Not to be dissing anyone, but London hip-hop is pretty much American hip-hop and it's Tricky and Massive that have changed that around a bit. I think that's why Bristol has got its own sound; it's not the kind of place you would immediately associate with Brooklyn. Like Tricky, he had that experience of living in that area, and he's been accepted because his nan's there and people have said "Oh he's okay, he went to school with one of us." He's fed up and bored and he'd go out and hang with these guys and it's a totally different mentality, the two sets, the black and the white, and to be between that, that leaves you with a different kind of thing, and a lot of times that's what he's captured on what he's doing, the sameness of each other, the black and white thing, and the differences as well; how he's caught in the middle. That's how a lot of it sounds to me, that kind of feeling of being caught up in something; it's not black, it's not white ... It's like hip-hop when it came out. You got into what they were doing and you got into that electronic music which was acceptable to anyone at any level, and into the energy of it, but you couldn't relate to the content because it was so American. The British experience is different, and Massive Attack, Tricky, Portishead and the jungle stuff that's happening now is more of a British, and more of a Bristol, thing.'

Growing up in Knowle, Tricky was also in contact with St Paul's, and with his father's brothers, who used to box (an attempt to emulate them led to Tricky's broken nose). The father himself remained absent, though there was occasional contact. 'I didn't see him again until I was twelve', he has said. 'I was looking through the phone book one day and I saw my name. My auntie said "That's your dad." So I phoned him up and said "It's your son." We met the next weekend and I saw him four times after that. The last time I saw him was at a club in St Paul's, with his mates. That was weird. It was like seeing a mate from school. He'd be smoking a spliff with a woman. He's a ladies' man, still, to this day.'

Hip-Hop Days

Like the other members of the Bristol scene, Tricky was transfixed by the arrival of hip-hop. Too late for punk, he had become a two-tone kid in the days of the Specials and the Beat, and he was already practising rhymes as a reggae-style toaster: 'I was waiting my turn', he says. 'I used to toast with a sound system run by a guy called Shockwave when I was fifteen. I would get calls saying the Wild Bunch were playing and to come and lay down some rhymes. I was following American rappers like Rakim and Slick Rick but I think I invented the English mellow style of rapping.' He was also hanging out with his South Bristol mates who had formed another posse, the Fresh Four, that went on to have a top-ten hit with the Smith and Mighty-produced version of the old Rose Royce tune 'Wishing on a Star' in 1989. 'He used to be in the Fresh Four early on', remembers Flynn, 'sort of in the late Wild Bunch days, and then he shot off and did that, and we carried on doing the DJ thing. We used to mix for him when he was MCing and we used to rap together. It was him that got me thinking about doing "Wishing On a Star", 'cos he was doing a little track himself and I thought "yeah, I like that".'

'I was always rapping', Tricky says, 'from way back. Do an insurance job on some turntables, get hold of some mikes, set up in a squat and you're away ...' He was also assembling a reputation as a bit of a nutter. 'I'm that pissed-up geezer that annoys you in pubs', he says, and anyone who has seen him come into a club, at least in his earlier days, would agree. He immediately tried to be the centre of attention, desperate to get a response, any response, spending hours chatting up girls, manically craning his head around the room to check out the action, like a hyperactive kid taken to a disco for the first time and finding the experience rather too over-stimulating. He was also a bit of a rough lot, getting into fights and causing havoc, though he was never a hard man, his size and asthma counting against him. 'I don't believe in turning the other cheek', he says. 'I do whatever I have to to stay true to what I believe.' When I ask him what he believes, he's momentarily lost for words. 'Er, I don't know!', he says laughing. 'But I know what I don't believe in: selling drugs like cocaine, prostitution, pimps, guys who think they're bad boys, that kind of stuff.'

Martina

Famously, it's said that Tricky met his singer Martina when she was sitting on a wall outside the house he was sharing with Mark Stewart, she a schoolgirl having a fag break in between revising for her GCSEs at Clifton College. On the album, Martina provides the perfect vehicle for Tricky's words, her blank, un-inflected voice carrying the songs into a territory his own whispered drawl would, on its own, make too samey, its menace becoming diminished (like the figure of the shark in *Jaws*), by too much familiarity. Instead her vocal naivety gives the noxious lyrics a disingenuous air of normality, and allows him to under-pin her featured numbers with ruminative, almost inaudible, raps, their long-drawn-out syllables savoured like Count Dracula rolling a fresh glass of blood around his mouth preparatory to swallowing it.

Tricky's rise to fame was, even before the release of the album, almost inevitable. Through careful management by Island, his record company, previews of the album were circulated to journalists at the end of 1994 and they convincingly made him their new face for 1995 in the end of year 'Whither rock?' pieces. When *Maxinquaye* was released to more or less universal acclaim the hype was such that the album already seemed a known quantity; the predictions had merely come true. The problem of how to translate a sample-deck form of music into a live show was tackled boldly straight away by setting Tricky up with a band of seasoned session musicians directed by ex-Boomtown Rat Pete Briquette, and sending him off on a tour supporting PJ Harvey, a convenient Island label mate, and one guaranteed to introduce him to an audience far wider than that normally commanded by a dance act. The conjunction of indie teen queen and the newly-made-up slapper rapper (a judicious touch of warpaint added to those gaunt features) was an early indication that Tricky was being seen as a very marketable commodity, to be sold as a product whose shelf space spanned the racks, rather than simply as a dance or R&B staple, whose limited appeal tended to attract cult success and relative facelessness in the media.

Tricky Live

Though the early performances were tentative, and Tricky on the road was a mass of nerves, the Massive Attack problem of how to distribute the music live was successfully confronted. No hiding behind turntables and MCs for Tricky, but quick, painful and immediate exposure to the rigours of the road and the privations of a second-on-the-bill attraction. No matter that he had no

(OPPOSITE)   Tricky on stage in Birmingham, 1995 (*photo*: Doug Smith)

real training in performance, beyond rapping on the mike at party jams; he was suddenly out there, people were paying to see him, and even if they had really paid to see Harvey they were being shown something new and might end up buying the album. On the tour he headlined one concert at Shepherd's Bush Empire, reviving the Bristolian connection which he had largely dismissed as irrelevant, by calling upon Smith and Mighty to support him. 'We went up to the gig with Smith and Mighty', remembers Flynn. 'We hadn't seen Tricky for ages so we had a real good time, and seeing his show was incredible.' 'It was amazing to see him so together', says Flora. 'You know he's so crazy anyway, like that's how he is, but he just went out there and was so professional. We were, like, stunned.' This was also the gig where he asked the audience if they wanted trip-hop. They cheered in assent as he rebuked them with: 'You can all fuck off then.'

Meanwhile, Tricky's period of adjustment to fame was proving a difficult one. He dissed his Bristol colleagues at every opportunity, slagging off Massive Attack and particularly Portishead in interview after interview. 'They talk about Massive Attack as my peers', he told me bitterly, 'but it's bollocks. I've been doing this for ages. My peers are Terry Hall of the Specials and Rakim.' He had a child with singer Martina, a daughter, Maisey, but any likelihood of connubial bliss was dashed by publicity surrounding an affair with Björk, and it seemed that for a time Tricky was becoming true to the promise of his slapper make-up; he was anybody's. He was also very stoned, the spliff count going up impressively from interview to interview. But he was also being unusually prolific, going off to Jamaica in early 1996 to record his next album whilst finding time for a side project as 'Nearly God' on his own Durban Poison label – part of an agreement with Island that he could continue to release products under different names.

Nearly God

Released in April of 1996, *Nearly God* was very well received, getting a five-star review from *The Guardian*. On reflection, it's only intermittently successful, half-completed tunes done in demo mode and varying from the inspired to the woefully inadequate, like Bob Dylan's *Self Portrait* done in trip-hop mode. But it's also impressively experimental and points towards a possible future far beyond the dreams of his peers, where Tricky could do anything, going not only beyond the usual restraints of a dance-music producer or the run-of- the-mill pop star, but moving into the realm of the international avant-garde. He could, you think, collaborate with Robert Wilson on a theatre piece, or compose string quartets for a work with Brian Eno or David Byrne, set dances by Twyla Tharp, soundtrack a Damien Hirst movie (providing, of course, that he could get a handy engineer to sort all the bits out afterwards). Alternatively, of course, he could also die before any of this could be accomplished.

On *Nearly God*, the musical settings are rougher than rough, repeated sampled loops doing little to disguise the vinyl scratches of their origins, or the cynical, bash-it-down-regardless ethic of the recording process. When Tricky deigns to do a vocal (most of the songs are fronted by collaborators, including Martina, Terry Hall of the Specials, Neneh Cherry – Tricky possibly reclaiming the work he did for her third album after his success rendered it unnecessary – and Björk), he sounds more than ever like a stoned white rocker, Alan Vega of Suicide for instance, than the supposed dance music icon he began by being promoted as. Some contributions – like the vocal by Alison Moyet on 'Make a Change' – are simply embarrassing, but the last song on the album, 'Yoga', sung by Björk, is a marvel – minimal but stark and beautiful – and as compelling as anything she or he has done. What his overall contribution was though, is open to debate. Terry Hall, who contributed to two songs on the album, was generally amazed, as well as inspired, by the speed with which the project was dispatched.

TERRY HALL

The press officer from my record company played me bits and bobs of Tricky's album in his office, and he showed me this article in which Tricky said he was influenced by my stuff, though he also said he thought I couldn't sing which I found funny. I tried to get hold of him and he tried to get hold of me and this went on for ages, until one night he phoned me at about 3a.m. and said 'It's Tricky', and I told him I'm not used to being called at three in the morning. But eventually we met up and had a coffee and there was this silence for about an hour, a really good, sussing-out silence that I do with everybody but he was doing back to me. I had thought that his music sounded pretty odd. I liked his lyrics and to me they didn't sound like black dance music, which is the bag he's been put into. I also saw a photo of him in a dress and then it sounded even less like black dance music.

The collaboration started by a nice sort of accident, I just wanted to know what he was up to and he was telling me how much the first Specials album had meant to him. Then two months later he had this idea for *Nearly God*, and I don't think he was sure what he wanted, he just had the idea of booking the studio with people that he liked, getting together to see what happened. I took this thing called 'Promised Me Poems' which I was going to use for my last album but it never fitted in. I never sing anything unless I'm sure it's going to be good, because the lyrics are so personal, but I just sang it straight off. What I discovered within half an hour of being in a working situation with him was that his attention span is so tiny, so incredibly short, that he would not even consider doing a second take unless the mike exploded or a horse wandered into the studio. I really liked that because it was going back to what made me get involved with music in the first place, the instant appeal of punk rock or whatever; you just go and do it, and whatever happens, happens.

Previously, he'd sent me rhythm ideas that were so mad that you couldn't even hum to them. He played me one – I think the one that Björk ended up on, which shows you where her head is at – where I couldn't even hum a bar of it, it was so cock–eyed. But overall the experience was pretty inspiring. I've made like ten albums and been through that whole eighties thing where everything went totally wonky and I got caught up in that thing of making sterile–sounding records. With Tricky it was pretty much like what the intention was in the Specials, which was a reaction against all those polished records. The first group I was in we didn't even have songs or proper instruments. The important thing is to deal with something that you think you should do.

Tricky Business

The Insects – collaborators with Massive Attack – also worked with Tricky on *Maxinquaye*, and they supply an intriguing insight into his methods of recording. 'We started to work with him on the album', says Tim Norfolk, 'but he and Massive were having a bit of a wrangle at the time and we got chewed up between them. I don't know whether he thought we'd be going back to Massive and telling them what he was up to, or the other way round. But working with Tricky was brilliant musically, just in terms of how to listen to the music, it was like adjusting your ears, a new way of listening, of doing things differently. There's not a lot that normal Bristol musos can show us, at least in terms of recording, but with Tricky it was more like how to listen and be creative. We worked on the track 'Pumpkin' with him and Alison Goldblatt, and we were at his flat and she came in and he just set up the mike in the hall and had her sing, mainly wordless noises. Then she said "Alright, when do we start?", and he said that was it, he'd done it.' 'I remember he played us "Ponderosa" when he'd just done it', says Bob Locke, 'and we said "That's brilliant, when are you going to finish it?", and he said it was finished. He was even going to master it from a cassette.'

After Tricky said in an interview that he had done all the music on *Maxinquaye* himself, the Insects sent him a postcard reminding him of their contribution, which didn't go down well, as he immediately phoned up about it, very angry. Paul Johnson remembers being at home one day, an anecdote which begins with the inevitable Bristol refrain 'I was just rolling a spliff when ...', and hearing a familiar tune from the television, which was tuned to *The Chart Show*. He went next door to watch it, saw it was Tricky and recalled the bass line he heard was one he claims he had contributed to a piece of music years ago, when Tricky and Mark Stewart had come round to his place to get some weed.

Tricky Symbol

If Tricky answered a need in the discourses of pop culture of the mid-nineties, and he surely did, it had to be as a sort of Nick Cave with dance credentials, part of a newly-deracinated ideal of angst normally answered by white singer/songwriters with serious drug problems. After all, dance music was now where it was at, the principal cutting-edge genre of the time, and if the times threw up a figure who appeared to come from the lineage of hip-hop yet who strived to express himself as a tortured artist of the type normally associated with the indie pop of Morrissey, then so be it; after all, this was too good a chance to pass up. Tricky was therefore given enough critical rope to hang himself several times over, and to engage Martina in a fashionable bout of bondage while he was at it. For black artists (and Tricky, for all the deracination involved in his promotion, was un-avoidably black) weren't supposed to behave in this way – being experimental, revealing themselves in

(OPPOSITE PAGE) Tricky and Spiderman (*photo:* Beezer)

their songs, playing up to the auteur theory of the solo artist by continually exposing their scars and wounds. If they did so, it was meant to be in code, like Prince, whose continual reinventions of himself never quite threatened the sense that you really knew who he was all the time: a Minneapolis genius-hustler who took on the skins of all of his forebears – Little Richard, Hendrix et al – but who, at rock bottom, remained an essentially carnivalesque hero of a type we knew about and could deal with. No, Tricky was something else; he was so much on the surface, his personality so imminent, and so disturbed, that he was genuinely dangerous.

The danger also spilled over into his personal life, or at least the mediated version of it supplied by inter-views with the press. When the writer for a *Face* interview guessed that relations between Tricky and Martina – who were, it seemed, no longer lovers, though they had a child to bring up – had assumed an air of conflict, especially over the arrangements for childcare of Maisey, Tricky hit the roof, confessing to *Time Out* that he would like to get hold of the writer and waste him. Even the *Bristol Evening Post* picked up the story, reporting that Adrian Thaws was going to move to America to escape the unwanted press attention. A soap opera of sorts therefore developed about Tricky's private life, although by now it wasn't very private anyway. In the *Time Out* article, it was revealed that Tricks was a big Michael Jackson fan, and obviously completely unaware of the inappropriateness of this enthusiasm in terms of his new-found rock credibility (what is worse, he also held a torch for the songs of Neil Diamond). Details of Martina – until now a fairly shadowy muse, the schoolgirl who had shucked off her privileged background to sing dirty ditties for vampire Tricks – also became known at last. She was ennobled with a surname, double-barrelled to boot – Martina Topley-Bird – and revealed as coming from a top-drawer family with links to the advertising business.

Tricky at Glastonbury (*photo*: Paul Box)

Marina had also asserted herself in her role as part of the recording unit known as Tricky, which was meant to include her but often didn't, by virtue of people naturally identifying the trademark with the person who bore its name. Her contributions to *Nearly God* were among the most effective of the whole project, and it began to seem that she was far more important than had previously been guessed at, the disconnected, posh–girl voice supplying a considerable proportion of Tricky's tricks.

The genius of Tricky, if that isn't too strong a term to use about a doped–up blagger from Knowle West, is that he, alone of all the Bristol-sound artists, really seems to have escaped the confines of his own background, to have slipped through the bars of the prison and successfully reinvented himself as a genuine star, able to do anything he wants, in any form, and still make it credible. He may be on a fast-burning fuse, and it's difficult to imagine him twenty years on (ten years, five years even, in fact it will be a surprise if he's still alive next year), but the promise of *Maxinquaye* and *Nearly God* is such that you don't know what he will do next, and are therefore enthralled at the prospect of whatever nameless weirdness he will put his name to. More than anything, he answers the carping muso criticisms of 'He can't play, can he?' It's the very fact that he can't play that makes him so interesting, for he just has to make it up as he goes along, blagging it, in the great Bristol fashion, and continuing to explore what he doesn't already know, which, more or less, is everything. Like Chatterton, he's reinventing a language that doesn't exist. Going back to the Tricky of *Blue Lines*, suddenly he doesn't sound so naive any more:

> It's a beautiful day, well it seems as such
> Beautiful thoughts mean I dream too much
> Even if I told you you still would not know me
> Tricky never does, Adrian mostly gets lonely
> How we live in this existence just being
> English upbringing, background Caribbean.

PORTISHEAD

If Tricky is dysfunctional, paranoid, a precociously disturbed young man, Geoff Barrow of Portishead may well be his dangerously normal twin brother, (in music if not in life). Tricky's first solo recording was made with Barrow, in the shape of the wonderful track 'Nothing's Clear', released on the Bristol charity album *The Hard Sell* under Tricky's name, with Barrow listed as co-producer, and described in the last chapter. But if Tricky is a son of the city, from one of the hardest estates in Bristol, Barrow is from the completely different world of the softie commuter suburbs, from, indeed, Portishead itself.

Portishead's Portishead

Or at least he spent his teenage years in Portishead, moving there with his mum from the seaside resort of Weston-super-Mare further down the coast after his parents split up when he was thirteen. A small dormitory town on the muddy shore of the Bristol Channel, just across the Avon from the fetid chimneys, chemical factories and marvellous *Eraserhead*-like industrial warehouses of Bristol's port Avonmouth, Portishead, with its optimistic seaside promenade fronting the seal-grey mud and opaque, polluted water of the channel, is a strange sort of place, so normal as to almost count as weird, in a *Blue Velvet* kind of way.

Though like Clevedon just down the coast, it made

attempts at being a seaside resort in the late nineteenth century, Portishead has more or less ceded any hopes it may have had in that direction; after all, you certainly wouldn't want to swim here, not with what goes into that water. There is the prom, though, and a pretty seafront boating lake and a café selling tea and cakes. Right on the edge of Battery Point, which John Cabot sailed round on his voyage to Newfoundland in 1497, lies the rather splendidly-decayed thirties lido, which still functions in the summer and over whose low perimeter walls generations of Portishead youth have climbed at dead of summer night to swim illegally or sit and sip their cider. Up from the pool is a wonderful bit of coastal woodland full of fossils, and back towards the town an impressive Victorian terrace that testifies to the town's one-time grandeur, though now the houses face a row of modern, sixties semis across the street.

Following the terrace downhill you eventually hit the town centre, what there is of it. There's more estate agents' offices than seems either wise or probable among the usual high-street shops and pubs, and the pleasing oddity of a thirties garage and petrol station in the shape of a half-beamed mock tudor house is miraculously still going. On a Sunday afternoon in spring the place is almost deserted apart from a few kiddies with skateboards walking about looking vaguely resentful, their industrial-size trainers kicking at the ground as they go about their business. A few years ago, Geoff Barrow could have been one of them. And that's about it, apart from the houses on the modern estates that ring the town on all sides, classic commuter-belt homes, thousands of them, in little drives and closes and cul-de-sacs of the kind you see all over the country. You can certainly make a good case for the promotion of the sinister and the exotic if you come from Portishead.

Portishead: Geoff Barrow and Beth Gibbons in an early publicity shot (*photo*: Martyn Goodacre)

On Friday and Saturday nights though, especially in the summer, the place does become a little wild at heart, with cider-head teenagers whooping it up after the pubs close. Portishead even had its own little riot once, when the carousing youths went mental and police reinforcements were sent for to Bristol. A white riot, it had no real cause other than drunkenness, boredom and the usual resentment at the police, and though the civic powers deplored it and there was much wringing of hands, it could happen again on any Friday or Saturday, if the temperature or the boredom index hits a high. Pleasingly for a band who have successfully denatured themselves from their origins in the suburbs (Barrow) and the West Country pub-rock and jazz scene (the others), Portishead the group received a jolting reminder of their origins when they played a show in San Francisco in 1995 and amid the rather precious stage atmosphere of gloom, doom and intensely delivered chanson, a rich yokel voice called out, right in the quietest bit of one of their songs, 'Drink up ye cider!'

Dummy

In the hundreds of articles about the group since their debut album *Dummy* was released to universal acclaim in 1994, the fundamental facts of the Portishead story have been repeated so often that they have begun to resemble the rather wearily-recited stages of a catechism:

1. Producer-boffin Barrow, who has worked as a tape operator and tea boy in the Coach House studio used by Massive Attack on their *Blue Lines* album, meets singer Beth Gibbons at an enterprise allowance day for the unemployed.

2. Beth has songs, Geoff has music; they agree to collaborate.

3. They are joined by shady back-room knob twiddler Dave McDonald and jazz guitarist Adrian Utley.

4. *Dummy* emerges fully-formed into the world.

5. The band appears on the television pop show *Later*, performing two songs. So shocked that the group can actually play, everyone who hasn't already bought the album immediately goes out and buys it.

6. Beth will not talk to the press. Geoff will, but he won't be photographed.

7. *Dummy* sells over one and a half million copies worldwide.

The successful creation of a myth of mystique out of what was, in essence, a bunch of normal musicians, looks now, after the fact, like a public relations master stroke. If Beth couldn't talk, she couldn't tell all about her background in various pub-rock bands of a kind similar to Airbus, with whom she performed a version of a Portishead track at Bristol's annual Ashton Court community festival in 1993. The focus on the two front runners also disguised the contribution of Adrian Utley, the guitarist, co-writer and co-producer, who was a very known quantity. Perhaps the best jazz guitarist in the country, he had been playing locally for years as a mainstay of the busy Bristol and Bath modern-jazz scene out of which he drew the other members of the Portishead live band, drummer Clive Deamer, pianist John Baggott and bassist Jim Barr. Gary Baldwin, who plays Hammond organ on *Dummy*, was also a colleague of Utley's when they both played in the neo-bop Tommy Chase band in the late eighties. Utley and drummer Deamer go back as far as the Glee Club, a local jump, jive and country boogie band from the mid eighties, and both had played with the R&B revival band the Big Town Playboys, backing guitar hero Jeff Beck on various tours. Utley also played regularly with Bath blues guitarist Kevin Brown, with whom he toured America a number of times, and he had run an occasional house rhythm section at Bristol jazz pub the Albert Inn, backing up visiting soloists like Jean Toussaint and Gerard Presencer, as well as playing behind US Hammond organ maestro Big John Patton on *The Face* magazine's Jazz Bop tour of 1989.

Utley was also a well-known local record producer, a habitué of the Coach House, where he worked on singles by the briefly successful local group Like Young, who featured his previous Glee Club colleague Stig Manly, now of Crustation, the current Bristol group-most-likely-to. Geoff Barrow, who got his job as an apprentice tape operator at the Coach House after helping to do some building work there, was also connected with the local scene, travelling on tour with Bristol skate-punk band the Seers, and later recruited to the Neneh Cherry/Cameron McVey axis which was so influential in the creation of the Bristol sound, writing material for Cherry's *Homebrew* album, as Robert Del Naja had done on her previous album.

Porter's Head

It was via the Cherry connection that Portishead got what was probably their first real name check, when a *Billboard* magazine profile of Cherry in 1992 mentioned Porter's Head, 'an unsigned Bristol band', who collaborated on the 'pensive and sullen "Somedays"' – from her second album *Homebrew*. It was the Cherry connection which brought Barrow to the attention of Go Beat records' Ferdy Unger-Hamilton, who subsequently signed Portishead. He then called Caroline Killoury and the group was recruited to her management company, Fruit, along with Tricky and Massive Attack, before Massive found new management.

The marketing of Portishead as a dance act was also a very successful move. Listening to *Dummy* now, in June 1996, the dance elements seem to have receded somewhat, although various remixes were much more hip-hop oriented. Instead, what strikes you is the concept of mood music with lovelorn lyrics that, given a different treatment, could have graced a thousand indie bedsit bands. The languorous late-night feel of the album comes essentially from jazz and torch songs, familiar from countless female-vocalist sets, a fifties Julie London soundscape. The instrumentation relies heavily on a slowed-down rare-groove aesthetic of easy, loping rhythms and guitar chords, with Fender Rhodes piano, Hammond organ, and the sampled-Isaac-Hayes strings on 'Glory Box' recalling sensual soul, and made contemporary by the hip-hop scratches and carefully distressed production sound, which is quite brilliantly realized for such a low-budget recording. But it was the hip-hop elements that caught everyone's attention, along with the sparing parodies of soundtrack albums (including a *Mission Impossible* sample) that hinted at a sixties James Bond/John Barry homage, and the group's film noir visuals and intimate chanson style. 'Isn't it just like you British', Verve jazz producer Guy Eckstine told me at a music business fair in Atlanta, 'to take something so essentially happy and upbeat as hip-hop, and make it all damp and foggy, like Portishead.'

The manipulation of the hip-hop beats, sometimes recorded from the music of the studio musicians and then scratched back into the mix from acetate discs, is what gives *Dummy* its dance credibility, such as it is, the eerie, timeless feel and crusty, ravaged quality – from the fissured surface of the plastic discs reworked into the songs – acting as a mark of authenticity. Otherwise, it's dangerously close to another indie angst album. 'Wandering star ...', one hears, and the plodding beat can suddenly sound as tired and as calculated as any rock band demo, though the quality

Portishead's only Bristol gig, at New Trinity centre in 1995. From left: Adrian Utley, Beth Gibbons, Geoff Barrow, Clive Deamer, John Baggott (*photo*: Paul Box)

of both the songs and the production seemed impressively new. What, ironically, perhaps more than anything signalled Portishead's success, were the rock values signalled by the brooding vocals and the guitar heroics, which, however tastefully dispatched, allowed it to enter a world of mega sales where the reggae-derived slackness of Massive Attack's *Blue Lines* was more or less barred as too rootsy, too remote from rock's customary mode of address. This may be an unfair summation of *Dummy*, but really, it has to bear the stigma brought on by its success, as so familiar has the record become – played to within an inch of death on radio and as ambient mood music in cafés and bars – that it's difficult to feel sentimental about it any more. Even its makers can't bear to listen to it.

If Utley represents the guitar rock and Gibbons the indie angst, Barrow is the hip-hop kid, obsessed with the beats. As a teenager in his home town, he says, he missed out on his youth by being diverted into compulsive record scratching. His mate Andy Smith, now Portishead's DJ, would call round at his Portishead home and they'd stay up all night listening to a stack of records, and then sampling them. 'I wasn't the type of teenager who'd go out and get smashed, unfortunately', Barrow has said. 'I was more the type who would stay in and worry about world affairs, reading the teletext. Basically, being sixteen, seventeen, eighteen, just never happened for me.'

The Coach House Days

Charles Stewart, Mark Stewart's younger brother and half of the project Reborn who, after the success of Massive Attack and the first Bristol buzz that followed it, signed a contract with Island that resulted in one single and an album that was pulled before release, remembers recording at the Coach House when Barrow was working on his music. 'We were in the main room for a couple of months and Geoff was in the pool room there doing tracks for Cameron. He wasn't even on a wage from Cameron but he used to pay for the room and Geoff was on a youth opportunity scheme, so he used to get his thirty pound a week from them. He wasn't so much a tea boy, as he did some programming and stuff and he was working on material that had the possibility of being put forward for Neneh Cherry's album. Even on the early stuff he was working with the John Barry soundtrack themes, with drum patterns and funny *Kung Fu* scores. It just sounded like today's Mo' Wax stuff at that point ... it didn't have any of that guitary thing that made it seem weird, it was drum patterns and strings, and it wasn't too dissimilar from Cerrone or any of those seventies breaks really; that sound-track stuff has been quite a tried and tested formula for alternative hip-hop over the years. When he met Beth she seemed like some eighties version of Janis Joplin and at first that freaked him out.

'I was surprised that people were saying that it was really good, to be honest with you, because I hadn't heard anything for a while. I wasn't particularly surprised that it was successful, but I know that they went for the Go! Discs deal because although there wasn't much money – I think it was something like a fifty grand deal all-in, research, recording and every-thing, because the album was made anyway, and Go! Discs seemed pretty sussed. They had this idea to do the film (the first promo, *To Kill a Dead Man*) early and this indie-crossover guitar stuff.'

Trip-Hop Exports

Though Beth Gibbons won't speak to the British press (there are lots of comic moments in the Portishead press book where she blanks the writer of the piece, zooming off in her classic British sports car at the first

sign of an unhealthy journalistic interest), she does talk
to writers from abroad. I've managed to unearth a video
made for the British Council in 1995, which beats the
drum of the trip-hop export figures, hymning the
Bristol sound as a kind of official British pop culture for
the nineties, and in which Beth is pictured on Bristol's
dockside, talking about the image of Portishead.
Entitled *The New Music – the UK State of Pop* the programme begins with the title music of Pigbag, and it's
nice to see the band picking up another useful royalty.
'Radio One is so clued in to what is happening in British
pop that it's unbelievable', says Andy Parfitt, managing
editor of Radio One, the video's first talking head. 'We
don't have the same commercial pressures that our
rivals do so we can get behind a band like Portishead
and play them on mainstream radio, where our
commercial rivals would never do that, and we can give
them sufficient support through our special shows that
they eventually become accepted and take off, so public
service broadcasting and Radio One in Britain are all
tied in, dovetailed nicely.' One imagines Lord Reith
calling out 'Yo!' from the grave.

'I think there's the trip-hop thing', says Parfitt again,
asked about what's new and happening in British
music. 'Trip hop is very languid and loping, sort of like
big rhythm, drums and bass, and over the top of it
there's a lot of clever sampling, some of which is taken
from James Bond movies, some of it from old-
fashioned British movies of the forties. Sometimes
they put hiss tracks on to make things seem really
bizarre but fantastic, and you've got sounds like
Tricky, like Portishead, like Massive Attack – blimey,
they're all from Bristol actually, funnily enough.'

Derrick Green from China records takes over,
looking like a classic old-style industry mogul. 'In
terms of really cutting edge and deep underground,

(OPPOSITE PAGE) Beth Gibbons at New Trinity, her intimate, smoky-nightclub
style shrinking the venue to bedsit proportions (*photo*: Paul Box)

the trip-hop scene, this is where Britain is back to its brilliant best. It's right there in the most experimental and the deepest of the underground in youth culture.' Cut to Beth Gibbons, filmed on the dockside by the *Lochiel* vessel, once host to hip-hop jams. 'Are you part of any Bristol scene?', the American-voiced interviewer asks. 'No, I don't think so', Beth says, 'not particularly, because unlike our contemporaries, people like Massive, Geoff and I are totally boring people who stay at home. We're not club types, we're just slightly obsessed with our own individual things that we do in our music. The Bristol scene, whatever it is, I just imagine is slow. It is a kind of relaxed, very relaxed city, which is probably why people prefer it to London, and which is certainly why I prefer it.'

Cut back to Derrick Green: 'Glastonbury is just a couple of miles from Bristol (actually, more like thirty, Derrick) and it's created almost a South-West scene of born-again hippies and a whole sort of hippie scene that happened down in the South West and that does react to the music it likes which then develops a following before radio, television or the press get on to it.'

To Kill a Dead Man

The selling of Portishead was, even from the beginning, when they were an unknown and possibly unlikely commodity, handled with considerable wit and taste. To mark the relase of *Dummy* a number of mannequins were placed in a variety of London locations, marked with the letter 'P', like a surreal reminder of the sixties television series *The Prisoner*. 'They were a studio band making esoteric music who initially didn't want to play live and whose singer didn't want to do interviews', said Tony Crean, Go! Discs head of international sales. 'That's why we hit on the idea of putting highly-painted mannequin dummies at highly-visible traffic junctions around London on the day of release, which created a lot of news stories.'

Another step in the campaign was *To Kill a Dead Man*, the ten-minute promo film which received a limited showing in cinemas once the band had begun to take off. A brilliant idea, less brilliantly realized, it was directed by film-school graduate Alexander Hemming on a very low budget. *To Kill a Dead Man* is an homage to sixties spy cinema, which effectively finds roles for each member of the group. Barrow is an assassin, Gibbons a kidnapped dupe with Utley as her partner, whom Barrow appears to kill, and Dave McDonald is typecast as the heavy. Risibly inadequate in terms of funding, the black-and-white, shot-on-video, film nevertheless succeeds in identifying a persuasive visual style that matched the retro British film-noir feel of the soundtrack, which tied together a number of instrumental excerpts from the album. The film was later adapted into the video for 'Sour Times'.

What sealed Portishead's success, however, was their first ever live appearance, done for BBC 2's *Later* programme fronted by Jools Holland. Just the fact that the band could actually play was enough to impress, but the intimate setting, with Beth standing all hunched up in her sloppy-Joe jumper and smoking her trademark fag, and Barrow bent over the turntables doing something obscure with a mixer, was sufficiently compelling to create a buzz. Their later live showcases, at London's Eve club, and in Edinburgh and Paris, all of which were widely reviewed, deepened the feeling that the group was something special and could be apprehended in the context of a 'real' band, which most dance acts self-evidently couldn't.

Scenes from the short promotional film *To Kill a Dead Man*:
(ABOVE) Beth and iconic DS Citroen; (OPPOSITE) Dave McDonald typecast as a
heavy. (*photos*: Mike Lipscombe)

Adrian Utley

Though the rest of Portishead wouldn't talk to me, I did get to do an interview with Adrian Utley who though he isn't a signatory to the band's record contract, co-produced *Dummy* and is credited as co-composer with Barrow and Gibbons on most of the songs. As noted, he's a superb guitarist, specializing in jazz of the old fifties Blue Note school, and I had known him slightly for years through writing about jazz. We talked in Bristol's Mud Dock café, where at one point the sound system began to play what sounded like Portishead's 'Glory Box', though at length it turned out to be its illegitimate twin brother, Tricky's 'Hell is Round the Corner'.

ADRIAN

I moved to Bristol from Devon in 1986 and I came for the jazz. Andy Sheppard was here, playing with Klaunstance and his own band, who I would see at the King's Arms just around the corner from where I was living. I'd been playing summer seasons at Butlins, where I was band-leader for one year and so I had to write all the parts out. Coming from a place where the jazz was not very good, it was immensely exciting for me. Bristol was really happening for jazz, there was a lot going on and it was good quality. I felt frightened so it was good to go and sit in.

I answered an ad in *Venue* for a job that turned out to be Glee Club. I had to lie about my age because the ad said 'young guitar player' and I was twenty-nine, and I'd been in the band for about a year before I owned up and found out everyone else was the same age. With Glee Club I started to do arrangements, because I was really into Gil Evans and, though it's all so pathetic really, that's how you try and learn. For me it was a way of making a living and playing near enough the kind of music I wanted to play. Tommy Chase saw me playing at Glastonbury and

Adrian Utley at New Trinity. Perhaps the best jazz guitarist in the country, his rare grooves, fuzz-box obsessions and soundtrack enthusiasms helped to create Portishead's sound. (*photo*: Paul Box)

that led him to ask me to join his band. I'd read about him in *The Face* and stuff and to me it was another good move because I could make good money playing the kind of music that I nearly wanted to play.

I learned about recording by watching. I'd done loads of sessions but I never really got at the controls and I just became obsessed with it, plus I was getting bored with touring. I'd done disco sessions in the late seventies, had a reggae–type band that recorded an album's worth of stuff at Horizon, where the Specials used to record, and I was definitely into sound but then I went off into jazz, and it was all to do with harmonics and the whole culture of jazz. By now I think I've got enough of that and I've decided to stop. Every time I put on a John Coltrane record which was made in 1962 or whatever, I feel I can't get near that, and it's now thirty-odd years later, and I don't see any point in trying, so I'd like to make a mark in a different way. Jazz is so dear to me that I don't allow myself to listen to it too much; I remember playing a blues gig with the Big Town Playboys and then walking into the room upstairs and they were playing Hank Mobley. It sounds pretentious but it was like healing. I could hear a walking bass and a ride cymbal and it felt like I'd come home from this troubled, shitty world outside and back to my own bed.

My interest in the hip–hop thing came from Tribe Called Quest, which Mushroom played me, and which I liked because a lot of their sound was Blue Note, Grant Green samples and stuff, and that was around the time I met Geoff. I also liked the aggressive, urban sound of Public Enemy. At that time I was sharing a room at the Coach House and I was really interested in the fusion of hip hop and jazz but I couldn't really do it, although I had hundreds of beats. That's how Geoff and I got together really, I was making loads of trippy beats and playing jazz over them, but I never recorded it, I'd just sit there playing it incredibly loudly. There were no songs and people used to listen to it and say there was no way it could be done, even though now it's become a genre.

Geoff and I moved into the Coach House on the same day, after he'd just come back from London, and we developed a mutual respect for each other's stuff. He was upstairs and I was downstairs and we'd go to each other's rooms and talk and then he left and didn't have anywhere to go so he would hang out with me, and we'd work on stuff, just arsing about. It would be just a tape with a break on it, and we'd be just getting to know each other really, talking a lot and smoking millions of fags. I was in a huge learning curve about hip–hop because he'd been into it for years. He didn't miss electro and all the break-dancing stuff, that's where he comes from. Then he got a set up in another studio and that's when I went over and played guitar on 'Sour Times'. It was pretty near to its final version and he'd been working with Beth for over a year. Because he had tracks that were hanging about, we still kind of hung out and talked but by then he was getting record–company interest. He was putting the album together then and that's when he asked if I would produce it with him. And that's a sketchy role really, co-producer, because it's his band, his project, so it's difficult to define what I do. Then I started to get involved in all kinds of bits and bobs, bits of writing and learning about arranging and stuff. We also had a mutual interest in soundtracks, and that stuff is definitely something I brought into Portishead. Geoff was massively into sound-tracks and I was into Morricone and Nino Rota and all those sorts of things. That's what tied us together really, he had a knowledge of soundtracks and so did I, though he's a total hip–hop head really, and if you listen to his remixes they're pretty dangerous.

We listened to *Dummy* so endlessly at the time that I never wanted to hear it again. I don't think any of us play it very much. There was an awful lot of time spent on it though there are still things that we didn't get right, like an out–of–time piano on one track, so there's still a rough edge to it.

Portishead is a team that works together but Geoff is the boss and we all contribute what we contribute. With playing live there was a problem originally; we thought how the hell are we going to do it and I spent a lot of time working on it. I know a lot of musicians and we got all the local guys, friends of mine, and we put the whole thing together. We talked a lot about how the sound was going to be worked out and we learned a lot. We rehearsed well, and it wasn't the usual nebulous form of rehearsal because I'm very experienced with bands and all of the musicians were experienced. Beth was very easy, she just sang brilliantly straight away with no problem. We had a few problems soundwise, trying to get her loud enough without compromising what she wanted to do.

The *Later* television show was the first gig and we

rehearsed for a week for that and it was a nice buzz. We always knew it would be possible to play 'Glory Box' live and on the other tune we found other ways of doing it; I was playing with a screwdriver I think. We had no roadies and I was on my knees trying to sort out these wires when Jools Holland said 'Is everything all right?' We all felt really nervous but confident that we had something a little different. When Percy Sledge was playing, the director was going mad and dancing – typical BBC stuff – but when it eventually came on the telly we thought we'd won.

When we played gigs some of the stages were too small and our gear was so old, but we couldn't rehearse any more; you've got to play a couple of gigs before the whole thing takes its shape and there comes a point when you need people to play to. Because people were into the albums we got away with it first of all and it just got better the more we did it. Every gig we played at was good, people were there because they bought the record and they knew the words, which was quite a buzz in itself. Generally, people are looking at Beth and they're hearing the sounds, the songs are the same and I think we connected with them. The bigger the gigs, the more difficult it was because you start to get into a real showbiz scenario, with a fucking great snake-pit with all the photographers in it. Glastonbury this year was absolutely unbelievable, I was in tears at the response we got. We played the acoustic tent and we weren't advertised but word went round and about two hours before, the tent started to fill up and people couldn't get into the field, never mind the tent. When it went off it was deafening and when Beth came on it was unbelievable.

Overall, we worked as hard on the show as we did on the record, we didn't take it flippantly. We tried, we didn't just go out and say 'Fuck this, we can get away with it.' Geoff has a lot of say on the live show, but I've had so much experience in bands, it's like all those years paying off.

BACK TO THE FUTURE:

Smith and Mighty and Bristol Drum and Bass

In the narrative equivalent to a break-beat loop, trying to find a conclusion to the story so far of the Bristol sound ends up leading you back to its beginnings once again, scratching over the intervening years. The latest wave of music to come out of the city and make an impact on the world outside is the jungle or drum-and-bass sounds of producer Roni Size, who together with the other members of the Full Cycle records crew like DJ Krust and DJ Die and their contemporaries Flynn and Flora, has invented a new, notably relaxed and mellow, form of jungle. Though their music is startlingly new and radical, and there are no song structures in it as yet, both the sounds and the people who produce them have a lot in common with the first wave of Bristol hip-hop producers, especially Smith and Mighty, who so far have remained a rather shadowy presence in this book. In retrospect, Smith and Mighty are among the most important of the whole Bristol bunch, at least in terms of their influence, which has affected not only the other Bristol bands but the entire genre of British dance music in the nineties. They have yet to make it big - after it looked like they would become the first real stars of the Bristol scene way back when - but they are still producing cutting-edge music, which perhaps makes them more

Rob Smith (left) and Ray Mighty, in an abandoned house in St Paul's, 1987 (*photo*: Rob Scott)

relevant to a consideration of the present rather than a summary of the past.

Smith and Mighty

If you listen to 'Anyone (Who had a Heart)' from 1988 – if, that is, you can get hold of a copy, and even the people who made it aren't sure where to lay their hands on one – you're immediately confronted by one of the key texts of the Bristol sound. It has dated hardly at all, possibly because it was so little heard in the first place, though it was a big hit locally, and its crowded sound-world still hasn't really been assimilated by the mainstream. It's characterized by a mid-tempo pulse whose stuttering drum-machine rhythms are set against a synthesized bass figure which anticipates the sound of jungle by at least five years. The falsetto vocal, together with the listener's inevitable familiarity with the Bacharach and David song, are dislocated by the juddering 'oomph' break beats that cut up the tranquil surface of the docile melody, and by the sudden shifts of time and the disharmonies of the uncomplementary key signatures.

The tune is less a continuous narrative than a free-wheeling stop and start, one movement seeming to hold sway until another, quite dissimilar one jumps the queue and usurps it. It's pretty much bass and drums, both of them coming from machines, and ridden over by some ancient synth-string sounds and guitar samples, with a plaintive note added by singer Jackie Jackson's high, reedy voice. The chorus of cut-up, speeded-up, backing vocals adds another kind of alienation effect to the already disturbingly strange sound. It's absolutely brilliant, less commercial than Soul to Soul or early Massive Attack, but strikingly new and different, and perhaps the first fully-naturalized document of British hip-hop. It also ups the slack Bristol sound rhythms pioneered by Smith and Mighty's work on Mark Stewart's 'Stranger than Love' of the previous year into a bolder and more dance-friendly form.

It was the duo's second attempt at a Bacharach and David tune, for they also covered 'Walk On By' earlier in the same year, following a pattern established by the Wild Bunch's version of 'The Look of Love' in 1987. 'Cover' doesn't really ring true though, as the originals are so distressed by the manic beats and thundering bass that Burt himself would have a hard time recognizing them if he missed the introductory vocals. Released independently on their own Three Stripe label, the tunes got noticed sufficiently for corporate ears to waggle in Smith and Mighty's direction.

When, the following year, they produced a version of 'Wishing On a Star' for a Bristol rap crew, the Fresh Four, with a vocal added by Liz E, a local teacher, and it got into the charts, they were wooed by Virgin and Polygram, and decided eventually to go with Polygram's London records because they didn't like Virgin's Richard Branson for political reasons. And then nothing happened, other than their brilliant production on an album by their protégé Carlton, another high-voiced Bristol crooner, who had also sung on Massive Attack's first, independently recorded, single 'Any Love' of 1988, which Smith and Mighty co-produced. The Carlton album, *The Call is Strong*, which was released by London in 1990 but sank without trace quite undeservedly, is the great lost album of the Bristol sound. The track 'Love and Pain' in particular is strikingly beautiful, Carlton's warm falsetto (a dream of a recording voice) set to a yearning hip-hop ballad that is simply wonderful, though only a few of the other tracks measure up to its standard.

After that, for the remaining five years of their contract, nothing escaped Smith and Mighty 's corporate straitjacket into a proper release, although an album and single were recorded before being pulled by the record company at the last minute. There are differing opinions about this state of affairs. Ray

Mighty and Rob Smith proclaim their innocence, insisting that they were stiffed by the suits at head office, but there are others in Bristol who think uncharitably that they participated in the stiffing (though this may well be totally wrong), taking the money – as much as half-a-million pounds over the years – and then taking the piss, happily sitting back and looking forward to the day when they would be dropped and able to start again on their own terms. Whatever the reasons, they managed to resurface in 1995 with their own, independently-released version of the album Polygram had been sitting on, called by its original title of *Bass is Maternal*, though it was almost completely reworked. A largely instrumental dub set, it's quite brilliant but hopelessly uncommercial, which may be what they wanted at this stage, and it hasn't exactly set the world alight.

Visiting their studio in late 1995 – actually more of a room, with a turntable and a few bits of equipment lying around – at Steve Haley's Vision Factory in Redland, not much was happening, and it may well be Smith and Mighty who most fulfil the Bristol myth of musicians who spend their days rolling spliffs and avoiding work. Only Ray Mighty is present when I arrive, fiddling with a turntable and smoking a joint. He grew up in St Paul's, where his parents ran a blues dance in the basement of his house. He remembers lying in bed as a child, listening to the thump of the bass from the speakers downstairs make his bed shake. 'It was the only frequency powerful enough to get right to the top of the house', he says. As a teenager he was a punk, meeting Nellee Hooper and Miles Johnson at punk gigs in town, and he took a part in the St Paul's riot in 1980. Wanted by the police but leaving town before they could get to him, he was later mentioned in the trial arising from the disturbances.

He was also closer than most in the Bristol-sound scene to the criminal subculture of St Paul's, though this is a touchy subject. Music, says Mighty, a striking-looking dreadlocked man with green eyes and a shy, abstracted manner, 'was just something to do rather than hanging around the streets being destructive. You can't break the law forever and it seemed a rewarding thing to do.' The Bacharach singles were produced after they had seen the Wild Bunch at a jam at the Malcolm X centre in St Paul's doing their version of 'The Look of Love'. 'I thought yeah, this is hip, this is what I want to do', Mighty says. 'Tough, loud beats, the odd little sample and a vocal going on, slow, very rare groove with a dubby bass line in a stripped-back empty mix.' The Three Stripe posse that Smith and Mighty had worked in was more like a traditional reggae sound system than the Wild Bunch. While the Wild Bunch never owned their own system, always hiring speaker boxes and amplifiers, the Three Stripe crew had their own gear and therefore approximated to that ideal – expressed very well in the film *Babylon* – of the sound system as a focus for group identity and pride: there were roles for everyone, from mixers to box carriers, and a place in the national network of black sound crews (with whom Mighty had travelled out of Bristol to community centres in Gloucester, Birmingham and London since he was a boy).

As *Bass is Maternal* was about to be released, in late 1995, Smith and Mighty were preoccupied with the business of having to perform live to support their record. Tricky had asked them to support him at a show in London, which had gone well, and they were now preparing for a short tour. 'It's not something I ever thought of doing really', Mighty said of playing live. 'I did it before and I didn't really enjoy it. Getting up and entertaining people, it's never been my thing. I was in a band about ten years ago [Sweat, an 'apocalyptic funk band', formed with Smith, Paul Johnson and Rob Chant] and even then I hated every minute of it. It seems like the most totally unnatural thing to do; you get all these people staring at you. I like the other stuff that goes with

it: the travelling, the free food and getting into the club free, and the free drink, but actually getting up there, it's a hard one. But I'll put up with it if I have to to; it's only an hour out of the day.'

The London records experience was, he says, disheartening. 'They liked us, and I think they still do, or at least the A&R guy liked us, but he had bosses to please and he couldn't tell them this was going to be a sure-fire hit, so they held back. We didn't have anything that really jumped out as a single or that they could recoup their money on. Then they picked a single and took it as far as a week before it was supposed to come out. We did a video, did the press and some live things, and then they pulled it. We were telling them to put the album out and see what feedback they got and decide from that what single to release, and what mixes, but basically they were very rigid, saying "We want this track, these mixes", and we gave it them but they pulled it because we didn't get a high enough listing on the Radio One playlist, we got a D and they wanted a B or a C. It didn't happen and I think that was the final straw. I was disappointed but in a way I was half glad. I thought because it was on a major it would be hyped and people would criticize it. They send out press releases, really horrible and cheesy things and put you up against someone else. A major will just chuck money at it and if it had come out I'd have taken every review as like they'd bought it. If you do it off your own bat it's genuine, not like it's someone London's paid or dined.'

For the five years of the deal Smith and Mighty took part in a kind of corporate tennis match, passing mixes over the net only to have them returned. 'This was the part I didn't like the most', Mighty says. 'It was like going for a job interview every time. After a couple of years you don't know whether anything you're doing

(OPPOSITE)   A Smith and Mighty recording session at the Three Stripe studio in 1987: (TOP)   from left, singer Jackie Jackson, rapper Krissy Kriss, Rob Smith, Ray Mighty (*photos*: Rob Scott)

is any good or not. It's soul-destroying; your self-confidence just goes if someone's knocking you back all the time. Basically, their criticisms were that there weren't any strong enough singles, and that technically it might not be right, especially for America. It was sound quality too, they wanted everything sounding well-engineered and mixed, digital recording instead of these hard-sounding drums and woffly bass. They wanted something they could sell to everyone, but if they had put it out, other artists might have taken the label with a bit more respect. There might not have been a market for it, but things have come round and now there maybe is.'

The deal came about after the 'Wishing on a Star' hit, which, Mighty says, was 'just something lying around'. Their manager of the time, Erskine Chambers, went up to London and hawked it around, got the London deal, then took his percentage and departed, leaving them without any real influence. If they had been luckier they might have signed with Cameron McVey like Massive, as he was interested in them, but things didn't work out. At the same time, in a comedy of manners, they had Virgin offering them twice as much money, with a two-album deal guaranteed. 'But we didn't agree with Richard Branson', Mighty says. 'We'd never met him but we didn't like the thing he gave off of being Mrs Thatcher's ideal businessman. If you don't like your boss and you don't want to give him money, you shouldn't really be working for him. They even got him to ring us up to try and close the deal. He asked what we didn't like about him and we told him. Where we come from there's not a lot of work around and when someone starts saying you've got to get on your bike it's patronizing, especially from a guy like Branson. He said "No, you've got me all wrong, I've got nothing to do with the Conservative party, they hate me because I own a gay club, I don't give them any money, you've misunderstood me." He even got someone to bike over his autobiography for us to read.

I wish now that we'd signed with him, for the money at least, but we'd probably have had the same soul-destroying time.

'It probably went back to the punk thing, why we told Branson to fuck off. I was into that, the idea behind the whole thing and it's still there; a lot of people carry their morals from that time.' Rob Smith comes in, late, just as the interview is ending. 'It's more of a mates thing really', he says of their partnership. 'We started off in a band and then did the sound system at Glastonbury and places like that, ten years of having a laugh really. We tend to agree, eventually', he says of their working methods. 'We trust each other's judgement and each allows the other to go a little bit further, though we don't instantly recognize what the other is doing. We complement each other. The next thing we do can be something else', he says. 'We've been holding this record for five years and now we'll be free to be something different if we want. But if we want to do the same, we'll do the same.' 'You only get one chance with a major', chips in Mighty, 'and we blew it. We've been gone and come back again twice. Usually you don't even get a go once.'

Despite their lack of commercial success, Smith and Mighty have been important in moving the music on, and are significant precursors of the move from hip-hop to drum and bass. Now, Rob Smith collaborates on drum-and-bass releases for the More Rockers label, and they have worked with other local artists, like the Full Cycle posse and Flynn and Flora, who occasionally use their studio for mixing, as well as dub-reggae producers Henry and Louis, who have their own room in the Vision Factory. *Bass is Maternal* was a wonderful album, offering up a timely summary of the latter-day Bristol sound by mixing reggae loops and samples with elements of rave and jungle, but it doesn't conform to any commercial formula. To make matters worse, especially for their plans to tour as a live act, a couple of the album's guest vocalists are

unable to perform live, and may remain so for some time, as they are now in prison.

Bristol Jungle

In the hands of Full Cycle records producer Roni Size, his colleagues DJs Krust, Suv and Die, and Flynn and Flora, who record on their own Independent Dealers label, the normally rather programmatic format of jungle has become unusually expressive, echoing the reggae roots and trip-hop slackness of the earlier Bristol hip-hop producers. The typical sound is like wheels within wheels. On the outside rim the skittering drumbeats stutter madly along at 160 beats per minute, though there's never a simple, metronomic regularity to their measures. Instead, the snare patterns remain doggedly unorthodox, the machine's virtual drumstick rarely falling in exactly the same place twice, as if obeying a kind of indeterminacy principle. On the next rim the beat is halved to 80 beats per minute, propelled by a fat synthesized-bass sound, and this is the tempo at which people dance, if they dance at all. Further in still come odd samples and bits and bobs of this and that, snatches of movie dialogue, spacey synth chords, stereo pans, crackly vinyl surface noise leading into a battered Fender Rhodes loop, almost anything really, if it works. Further in than that, is the very heart of darkness – though it's difficult to know if what you are hearing isn't just an auditory illusion – of a loping reggae pulse and sundry dub shenanigans, or perhaps the slower than slow ghost of a slack trip-hop rhythm. The sound of Bristol jungle is unlike anything the rest of the country is producing, and, as with the previous generation of pioneering trip-hop producers, it's about to become world famous.

They're talking about Roni Size in Japan, in New York

(OPPOSITE)   Smith and Mighty supervising a recording session at their studio, 1987 (*photo*: Rob Scott)

and LA. Though his debut album for Talkin' Loud was at the time of writing still awaiting release, he's already an underground dance-music legend, and together with his compatriot producers he's part of a movement that is perhaps the most important new musical force of the moment. Its roots also go back into the golden age of Bristol hip-hop, pre-dating the emergence of Massive Attack, Tricky and Portishead, when in 1989 Krust and his brother Flynn (now half of Flynn and Flora, whose *Native Drums* album was released in April 1996) were part of the Fresh Four, whose Smith-and-Mighty-produced version of the old Rose Royce hit 'Wishing On a Star' made the top ten and got them an abortive deal with Virgin.

At the Full Cycle headquarters, Unit 23, Easton Business Centre, a shiny government-funded bulwark against the inner-city deprivation of downtown Bristol, the phone never stops ringing and the various mobiles of the principal partners are constantly pressed into service. Outside, a cameraman for a Channel-Four documentary bids Roni and Krust drive their battered saloon through the gates again and again to get a usable take. Inside, the sound of a trademark drum-loop jerks away unattended, as the DJs get themselves ready for the weekend's trip to Amsterdam. 'We've been to all kinds of countries', Krust says. 'France, Germany, Vienna ...' Die hands Roni a series of DAT tapes containing their latest mixes, to be taken to London for further consideration by Talkin' Loud. Their schedule is fuller than full; for two years Full Cycle have been putting out a single a month – a selection of which are collected on the album *Music Box: a New Era in Drum and Bass* – and until recently, when it was acrimoniously axed, Roni and Krust did a weekly radio show on the local station Galaxy, which became required listening, especially in the region's prisons whose residents' letters filled the

The Full Cycle posse: clockwise from top, Suv, Krust, Roni Size, Die
(*photo*: Jude Eddington)

postbag each week. Coaxed into an interview, Roni – a small young man with long, braided hair tied back into a ponytail – sighs and begins wearily to talk, shutting the door of the studio against the ringing of the phone and the constant swearing of Krust.

Roni Size

RONI

For me, what I was doing before, I can't really remember. I just remember making music and then people calling it jungle and then drum and bass. I've always been doing it, been in the studio for years, making reggae music, making soul, hip–hop, funk, everything that just filters through and we used to experiment with. But I worked out then that you had to be even better than the regular artists, or better than American hip–hop. You couldn't be British hip–hop because it wasn't your thing and you couldn't be reggae because you weren't Jamaican and it wasn't your thing either. We had house, but I wasn't into house, so I was always looking. So what was I looking for, before so–called jungle and drum and bass? I was looking for something which ... I used to run sound systems, I used to do DJing and I moved on to the studio side of things at the Basement project. They used to have a drum machine and I just used to play with it and then they got more and more stuff and I worked with it and knew how to use all of it, it was like a school. After real school – at Monk's Park, which I got threw out of – I went straight into the Basement. What happened was the rave stuff started to use a lot of break beats, but I didn't really like all of the sounds and because I liked reggae anyway, I used to like the warmth of the bass, I took the breaks from the hip–hop and the bass from the reggae and sped the rave up, so you came up with a different formula straight away. Then it became English and people started calling it jungle and then drum and bass. We were just mixing up beats and being experimental. You used to have English rap groups trying to identify with American groups but it wasn't for me. I used to like the beats but when it come to the lyrics and they started talking about 'I'm bad this', and gangster that and guns I wasn't into none of it so I moved on to instrumental music, and it was minimal and we were like minimalists.

When we was making *Music Box* me and Die used to call it ozone-friendly music, meaning that everyone would like it. The beats wouldn't be too aggressive, the bass would be warm and melodic, the sounds would be universal. We used to sit and say to each other, 'This is crossover music, you've got to like this'; we've studied it, and we try to generate interest by our choice of instruments, like we'll introduce a horn or a piano, or a reggae vocal or a hip-hop vocal – you just want to get people interested.

It's just me and Krust or me and Die, and you don't realize that you're doing it. You just do what you do, collecting all your favourite sounds, getting vibes from them and putting them in. If they fit, they fit; if they don't you save them for another day. It's just the actual selection of the sounds that you use and the way that you use them, and what you've learned in school, the tricks of the trade. It's just experimenting and seeing what happens, not doing anything out of the ordinary. It's not the equipment that we use or the sounds we have, it's about the vibe between us, and if I pick it up I go, 'Fucking hell, this is bad!' And if he goes, 'He's right you know, it's bad.' It's just the simplest things, and it comes from experience, like learning to drive or eat with chopsticks. As to the jazziness of it; to me jazz isn't a music, jazz is a progression and we're always progressing, we never use the same sound twice, we never use the same format.

Being from Bristol, we're not in a rush, we're just setting up the foundations, so that when it happens we're ready for it. There's no industry down here and MTV aren't going to come 120 miles for us, magazines say we need you now ... so I'm going to set up an industry down here, a building the size of that tower block over there, with recording studios, cutting rooms, distribution, a bar and restaurant for the people who work there, like we've got a sandwich machine at the moment. On a small scale we're doing exactly that here. It may not look like much but look, those speakers cost five grand.

Flynn and Flora

Flynn and Flora started to formulate their own form of jungle after travelling out to free parties as a sound system in the early nineties. 'We'd always been into

DJing and into the warehouse parties, where you could play anything, especially lots of heavy bass, and that's where it came from really', Flora says. 'After the warehouse thing died', Flynn takes over, 'the hip-hop sort of fizzled out and everyone got straight into rave. Everybody was trying that hip-hop thing so hard but it couldn't quite make it because it was so American, and then rave came out and suddenly boom! – everyone could get it, there was no lyrics and you could throw in all of these samples. We'd be going out in a big Transit with a load of friends at weekends, and the music at the raves was relevant to us because we understood the basis of sampling and we'd know that they were sampling certain bits, and that that sound was a 303 machine and that's an 808, so after that we'd be saying "that's the lick", this is where we had to be going, this is the latest

Flynn and Flora

thing. And then it was just a matter of sampling techniques getting better, editing techniques getting better.' 'And then the break-beat thing went into drum and bass', says Flora, 'while the kick thing went into heavy house and hardcore'. 'At the free-party scene the music translated into the feelings of a whole generation', says Flynn. 'To get that amount of people out at any given weekend was amazing, and you found something to relate to, and it didn't say anything! That was the biggest part of it, nothing was being said, but like check the vibe on that. Castle Morton broke the back, there was just too many people. It wasn't anything to do with hippies, peace and love and that. Everyone had a car and was told a place to go, and then another place. You got there late at night, eight of us in a van, looking around and getting that buzz, like boom!, the buzz that everyone else had. You'd just feel at home; it was like being able to take off your coat, relax, chill out, do whatever you want.'

They work with primitive equipment in their home, at the equivalent of the kitchen table, sampling as they go. 'It's very minimal', Flora says, 'very low budget. It's really weird because everyone else seems to have the right samplers, everyone has Akais or whatever these days, mad machines that can do everything, whereas ours is ancient, the sampling time's about fourteen seconds.' 'We take anything from anything', Flynn says, 'videos, tapes from friends, old records ...' Their album includes a wonderful snatch of alto sax, perhaps Charlie Parker, and a dialogue excerpt that came about because they mistakenly plugged the leads of the sampler into the telly instead of the video. 'We'd got the sample all lined up', says Flora, 'and then when we pressed the button this voice saying "You can pull this switch" came out from the telly. We just thought, yeah, we got to use that.'

Years ago, Flynn was part of the Fresh Four, along with Krust and Suv, who are now at Full Cycle, and Flora's brother Kosta was a friend of the Wild Bunch, running

The Fresh Four in 1989, with future stars of Bristol jungle, Flynn left, Krust (front), Judge back and Suv right.

Special K's café, which was a main hanging out place in the early days. 'We didn't make the music in the Fresh Four days', Flynn says, 'we just had an idea. Smith and Mighty really produced "Wishing On a Star", and we took a back seat. We were messing around with the turntables, mixing in the kitchen, and we found this loop with "The Funky Drummer" and "Riding High" by Faze-O, and we thought these two things sounded really good together and carried on mixing them on this tape. We had a record of "Wishing On a Star" by Rose Royce playing and we thought the lyrics would sound alright on this break, so we messed around with that idea for ages. Then we phoned Smith and Mighty up and went down to their studio on Ashley Road, played them the tape and said "What do you reckon?" They liked it but then it took about a year when we worked out the breaks, wrote a little bit of lyrics to go in-between and Flora knew a girl who could sing so we got Liz E in, and took it through a few more stages. Smith and Mighty's manager heard it, liked it and got us a deal, so we went with him.'

The Fresh Four's album was never released, and their manager, Erskine Chambers once again, took them for a ride. 'He was getting studios to make out receipts', says Flynn's brother Krust, 'saying we had used up more time than we had. But it was a crazy time, we would get five hundred pounds for playing a few records at a disco.' 'Some of the album was produced by Smith and Mighty, and some by the Fresh Four', Flynn says. 'Listening to it now, I'm sure Virgin thought it was too similar to what Massive were doing, it wasn't a straight Soul to Soul thing, which was probably what they were looking for. But it was a good learning experience. It's made us more independent now, knowing that we can do it ourselves. The reason we're on our own is that Full Cycle has a heavy roster with a lot of artists and a lot of tracks to put out. But their backgrounds aren't too dissimilar to ours; Bristol is a small town, and we just go with the sounds that seem right.'

AFTERWORD

So – as you imagine the trench-coated forties-film detective sifting through the evidence, picking up cassettes, CD boxes and eight-by-ten glossies, and examining the ashtrays with interest – where did the Bristol sound come from? Surely there is one, for how else do you account for the same tempos, the same samples, the same overall feel to much of the music coming out of the city from the mid- eighties to the mid-nineties? But how did the urgent rhythms of hip-hop become so slowed down, so relaxed, so (forgive the phrase) trip-hoppy? What made upbeat black American music devolve into mid-tempo skanking form, loosening up the breaks into the pulse of lover's rock? And what made it then change again, into Tricky's unique pick and mix of rap, rare groove and rock (though this makes it seem far less experimental than it is), Portishead's contemplative film-noir ballads, the later Massive Attack's sophisticated sci-fi soul, and Bristol jungle's soft centre?

For a start, hip-hop was never so monolithic, nor the Bristol sound so clichéd, as this view would suggest. The music of Tricky, for instance, is hardly relaxing, though it is often slow, and hip-hop always had a mellower side. But, to follow this line briefly, one possible answer lies in the extent to which hip-hop had permeated the city in the first place, the way it was taken up so wholeheartedly, and immediately appropriated into a subculture that also took in graffiti art, skate-boarding and all the other ingredients of an

integrated lifestyle, so that it colonized the suburbs as
well as the inner city, Portishead as well as St Paul's. The
alien form was naturalized into the structures of British
life, or life in the South West, which may well be lived at
a slightly slower pace than elsewhere, slower than in
London at least. As noted, Bristol couldn't really sustain
the sense of tension associated with Brooklyn or the
Bronx, and Bristolians were therefore forced to adapt
the new culture in accordance with their own needs.

For older kids, this culture was also imprinted on to
an earlier template, notably reggae, which had established itself because of the significant West- Indian
population in the city, and also because of its
associations with punk, which in Bristol had developed into a notably different form to elsewhere, more
intellectual and more responsive to black culture.
Reggae was the most popular music at club and party
scenes in the early and mid–eighties, and it offered a
glimpse of a hardcore hip lifestyle that was symbol-
ized in the imagined rootsiness of the blues dance in
St Paul's, acceptance at which became an aspiration for
many a young rebel disaffected by his or her own
culture. And in Bristol, St Paul's was just down the hill
from otherwise safe, middle–class homes. Black kids
who lived outside the area, in the estates or the
suburbs, still had relatives there and learned to see it
as a kind of focus for black life in the city, the centre
for sound systems and political and self–help groups.
And while most white kids interested in the new
music didn't go to St Paul's, they didn't have to; for
the first generation of producers at least, St Paul's
came to them at the Dug Out, whose overall ambience
was largely shaped by the city's black culture. Much
of what made the Bristol sound lies in this rub of
black and white, of city and suburb, of working and
middle classes, of punk roots and hip–hop aspir-
ations, levelled out by the pervasiveness of reggae.

In Bristol there was no dominant school serving the
areas with the most black residents, and the overall

cultural values were largely white Bristolian ones. Hip-hop attracted a multi-ethnic following of kids from everywhere, who were into the clothing, the styles and the related sports as much as the music, though for black kids it also offered a defining vision of racial identity. The little scenes that grew up, Tricky and the Fresh Four in Totterdown, Smith and Mighty in St Paul's, the Wild Bunch and Massive Attack round and about Montpelier, even Geoff Barrow and his mates out in Portishead, developed out of friendship and leisure pursuits as much as anything else, and when they began to make music there was no real commercial pressure applied from outside. They therefore had time to develop, even to start again from scratch, after they first began to make music.

There is also the question of a house style. Since the Wild Bunch's 'The Look of Love', Mark Stewart's appropriation of Smith and Mighty's 'Stranger Than Love', and Smith and Mighty's own 'Walk On By' and 'Anyone', a trademark had been established, a kind of stylistic signature, which became very influential in dictating what was to follow. Bristol is a small city and the people who produced the early hip-hop-derived records moved in the same circles, recorded with the same vocalists at the same studios, and had been open to the same influences and responsive to the same pressures. In nightclubs such as the Dug Out, no one danced very much and the dominant mode of listening was a reflective one, an ear cocked to the speakers of the sound system while the hand still held a joint or a drink. What moved people most was the sound of the bass, which could be received almost unconsciously, as in deep, dub reggae, providing a rhythm to live by rather than dance to, a pulse that could be internalized by the listener and attended to, if at all, at the level of the everyday, through nodding heads and tapping feet.

When the first productions of the Bristol sound quite naturally adapted this slower, heavier, lover's-rock-paced pulse – following the example of the Wild

Bunch sound-system in mixing reggae with funk and electro – an identity gradually emerged. That it stuck was perhaps a consequence of the relatively unformed structure of the music industry in the city; in fact there was hardly a music industry at all, and in the absence of pre-existing structures – especially when it came to making music from the new instruments of drum machines and turntables – the early producers had to make up the rules as they went along. And as they had virtually invented these new techniques for themselves in the creation of their sound, they were hardly likely to abandon them at the drop of a hat, or at the whim of a visiting A&R man, especially as they had internalized the rebellious attitudes of punk, and also, perhaps, the complacent heritage of their home city, which didn't put a false smile on its face for anyone if it could help it.

'It comes from people down here having time to work on stuff', says Charles Stewart. 'From them sitting on a product, with even the big boys not working to tight deadlines. I don't think this is a laid-back, spliffed-up, relaxed thing at all. I like to think it's intelligent, and also an irreverent attitude to the business, and why not? This city has never had a music business image, never had a pop reputation, so people's ideas about the industry remained fresh, whereas in Manchester you've got a whole legacy to live up to. If my brother has left any kind of a legacy, then I think it's one of doing things on your own terms.'

Certainly, the legacy of punk was a powerful one, both in terms of recording techniques ('bash it down!'), and business practice, and its values pervaded the efforts of the first hip-hop producers, and then filtered down to the second wave, with Tricky emerging as a significant Mark Stewart protégé. The way Tricky's music has moved far away from any received notion of hip-hop or dance, the way Portishead have crafted a new, dark and brooding sound to set Beth's lovelorn lyrics to, and how Massive have at last departed from their sound-system roots, emphasizes the willingness to experiment and take risks in the careers of the Bristol sound artists, and the courage not to merely follow fashion (which, anyway, they had created themselves, without even trying). Even the latest wave, the jungle of Roni Size and the others, is a reflection of this: a kind of anti-jungle, dance music you can't dance to, which instead recalls the slow pulse of reggae at its heart and an ambient, jazz-influenced, mode of listening.

Also, as mainly non-musicians (at least in the sense of being formally trained), the Bristol sound producers perhaps tended to hear the music first and foremost as sound, and learned to shape it accordingly, without much preciousness in their attitudes to the end-product, in the manner of real bands or instrumentalists anxious to keep their personal fingerprints on the text of the final track. By also working mainly in teams, their music is further removed from the sense of one, all-powerful, author-as-God kind of presence, and therefore more likely to soak up elements from the culture around them, like a good Hollywood genre movie.

In retrospect, the growth of a sound which is now known throughout the world, with a stylistic identity all of its own, is amazing, especially given the lack of any real musical success by Bristol in the past, excepting of course, good old Russ Conway. The next efforts of the principal producers - Massive's punk album, Tricky's next exposure of the heart up his sleeve, and Portishead's widely-awaited follow-up, are longed for with an intensity that few other groups could hope to achieve. And although it's the end of the story for this book, it's still really right at the beginning for the Bristol sound, which should continue to develop (slowly) for some years yet. Unless, of course, the curse of this book kills it off first.

SELECTED DISCOGRAPHY

I've chosen to list mainly albums and those items still in print, with a few crucial exceptions. Neither the Wild Bunch's 'The Look of Love' single from 1987 on Island nor Smith and Mighty's 'Walk On By' and 'Anyone' from 1988, on their own Three Stripe label, have been re-released.

The Pop Group (Gareth Sager, Bruce Smith, Mark Stewart, Simon Underwood, John Waddington):

Y (Radarscope Records, 1979, LP). The debut album, credited as produced by 'Dennis Blackbeard Bovelle and the Pop Group', with record sleeve by Rich Beale and Malcolm Garrett. Re-released on Radarscope CD 1996, with additional track 'She Is Beyond Good and Evil'.

For How Much Longer Do We Tolerate Mass Murder (Rough Trade, 1980, LP). Credited on the label as 'recorded and mixed Foel Studios by the Pop Group and Dave Anderson', with the legend 'Work, Buy, Consume, Die' imprinted on the label.

Rip Rig and Panic (Gareth Sager, Sean Oliver, Mark Springer, Bruce Smith with Neneh Cherry and Andrea Oliver as occasional vocalists):

God (Uh-Huh Productions for Virgin Records, 1981, LP). Comprising a 45rpm double album of four, colour-coded sides, and credited as

produced and composed by Rip Rig and Panic.
I Am Cold (Virgin Records, 1982, LP). Another
four-45rpm sides, this time East-West-
North-South, and featuring Don Cherry on two
tracks, with Steve Noble replacing Bruce Smith
on drums.

Mark Stewart:

Mark Stewart (Mute Records, 1987, CD). Excellent
solo album, produced by Adrian Sherwood and
Mark Stewart, with music by Doug Wimbish, Keith
LeBlanc and Skip McDonald. It includes the Eric
Satie/Smith and Mighty appropriation 'Stranger',
along with a second version entitled 'Stranger
Than Love', and a 'Stranger Than Love Dub'.

Carlton:

The Call is Strong (Three Stripe label, FFRR
Records, 1990, CD). Produced by Smith and
Mighty, this was the only album to result from
their five years with Polygram's London records.
Carlton's pure falsetto voice and sharp lyrics still
stand up well today, especially on the opening
track 'Cool With Nature', and the killer ballad
'Love and Pain'.

Massive Attack (Robert Del Naja, Grant Marshall,
Andrew Vowles with Horace Andy and Shara Nelson –
Blue Lines only – as vocalists):

'Any Love' (Massive Attack Records, 1988, 12"
single). Independently-released first recording,
credited as 'Featuring: Daddy Gee and Carlton'
and as 'produced by Massive Attack and Smith
and Mighty'. There are four mixes of the tune.

Blue Lines (A Wild Bunch recording, Circa
Records, 1991, CD). Credited to Massive ('Attack'

being dropped in deference to the terminology of Gulf War news reporting), and produced by Massive Attack with Johnny Dollar, executive producer Booga Bear (i.e Cameron McVey). The seminal debut album, with vocals by Shara Nelson, Horace Andy and Tony Bryan, and guest rapping by Tricky Kid and Claude Williams.

Protection (A Wild Bunch recording, Circa Records, 1994, CD). Credited as 'produced and mixed by Nellee Hooper and Massive Attack'. The long-awaited follow-up, featuring two tracks sung by Tracey Thorn to her own lyrics, raps by Tricky on two tracks, and two vocals by Nicolette, as well as two instrumentals and a version of The Doors' 'Light My Fire' sung by Horace Andy.

Portishead (Geoff Barrow, Beth Gibbons, with Dave McDonald and Adrian Utley):

Dummy (GoBeat!, 1994, CD). The debut album that sold a million and a half or more worldwide, and produced by Portishead with Adrian Utley.

Tricky:

Maxinquaye (Island Fourth and Broadway, 1995, CD). The crucial debut album, including the earlier singles 'Aftermath' and 'Ponderosa'.

Nearly God (Durban Poison, Island, 1996, CD). Not a Tricky album as such (or so his contract dictated), and credited to Nearly God, this is the famous collaboration with Terry Hall, Martina Topley Bird, Björk, Neneh Cherry, Alison Moyet and Cath Coffey.

Smith and Mighty:

Bass is Maternal (More Rockers, 1995, CD). The

come-back album (a double on LP), is a mainly-instrumental dub set, moving the Bristol sound on through rave to jungle, and full of heavy rocker's-reggae samples and beautifully-chosen, sparely-used vocals from a number of collaborators. The track 'Evolve' is particularly good.

Flynn and Flora:

Native Drums (Independent Dealers Records, 1996, CD). Home-made, heavy-on-the-sampler, low-budget, drum-and-bass set.

Henry and Louis:

Rudiments (More Rockers Records, 1995, CD). An hommage to seventies Jamaican dub, made largely through sampling, and produced by the 'two kings', aka Jack Lundy and Andy Scholes, working out of the same Vision Factory studio as Smith and Mighty.

Various:

The Hard Sell (Earth Recordings, 1991, CD). Bristol charity album produced in aid of OSCAR, a Sickle Cell Anaemia organization, and Airspace Charity, a movement, play-and-dance group. As well as containing the Tricky track 'Nothing's Clear', credited as 'produced and mixed by Tricky Kid and Geoff Barrow', the album also features a Massive Attack mix of Sean Oliver's 'Furious Fire' (Oliver, a member of Rip Rig and Panic, died in 1990), 'Loyalty is Valuable' by Mark Stewart and Tony Wrafter, 3PM's 'Manifestation', produced by Smith and Mighty, and 'Possession' by Charles Stewart's group Reborn, among the fourteen tracks.

Music Box: a New Era in Drum and Bass (Full

Cycle Records, 1996, CD). Credited as 'compiled by Roni Size' and featuring mixes by Scorpio, Roni Size, DJ Die, DJ Krust, and Bill Riley. The album presents the Bristol sound of deep drum and bass to great effect.

Cup of Tea – A Compilation (Cup of Tea, 1996, CD, LP). A collection of the latest wave of Bristol artists, many of whom, like Spaceways and Statik Sound System, almost pre-date Massive Attack, Tricky and Portishead.